PORTABLE CHEF

Baking

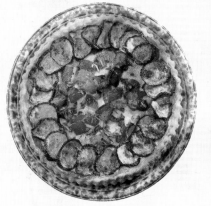

Emma Patmore

SMITHMARK

This edition published in 1998 by SMITHMARK Publishers,
a division of U.S. Media Holdings Inc.,
115 West 18th Street, New York, NY 10011.

SMITHMARK books are available for bulk purchase for sales promotion
and premium use. For details write or call the manager of special sales,
SMITHMARK Publishers, 115 West 18th Street, New York, NY 10011.

Produced by Haldane Mason, London

Acknowledgments
Art Director: Ron Samuels
Editorial Director: Sydney Francis
Managing Editor: Jo-Anne Cox
Editor: Felicity Jackson
Design: dap ltd
Photography: Iain Bagwell
Home Economist: Emma Patmore

ISBN: 0-7651-0874-7

Printed in China

10 9 8 7 6 5 4 3 2 1

Note
Unless otherwise stated, milk is assumed to be full fat, eggs are medium,
and pepper is freshly ground black pepper.

Contents

Introduction

This beautifully illustrated book brings you all the skills you need to re-create some of the best-loved traditional baking dishes. It also shows you how to experiment with some of the exciting new ingredients now readily available in most supermarkets.

Clear step-by-step instructions guide you through the techniques needed to master all those baking favorites that have been savored and enjoyed from generation to generation.

PUDDINGS & PASTRIES

Experience the sweet pleasure of a wonderful selection of everyday and special occasion desserts in Chapter 1 as it shows you how to make rich, sticky, and irresistible desserts, such as Pavlova, Fruit Crumble, Queen of Puddings, and tasty chocolate puddings. Everyone's favorite is sure to be included.

This chapter also helps you to perfect your pastry so that you are guaranteed success with such timeless classics as Syrup Tart, Apricot & Cranberry Frangipane, Apple Tart Tatin, Custard Tart, and Cheese & Apple Tart.

BREADS & SIDE DISHES

Making bread at home is great fun and allows you to experiment with all sorts of ingredients, such as sun-dried tomatoes, garlic, mangoes, and olive oil, to create versatile and delicious variations of modern breads, rolls, and loaves. Chapter 2 also shows you how to spice up all sorts of side dishes with exciting adaptations of traditional flans, pies, and scones, such as Cheese & Mustard Scones, tasty Cheese Pudding, Onion Tart, and delicious Celery & Onion Pies.

VEGETARIAN COOKING

Vegetarian recipes full of delicious wholesome ingredients, which are every bit as good as traditional baking favorites, have been created in Chapter 3. Recipes include Lentil & Red Bell Pepper Flan, Date & Apricot Tart, Pineapple Upside-down Cake, and Brazil Nut & Mushroom Pie.

CAKES & COOKIES

Transform traditional cakes and cookies into a real extravaganza with some new adaptations of old favorites in Chapters 4 and 5. Irresistible cake recipes, such as Marbled Chocolate Cake, Olive Oil Fruit & Nut Cake, Gingerbread, and Meringues, are included as are delicious cookie recipes, such as Chocolate Chip Cookies and Gingernuts. These recipes are quick and easy to make and will delight the whole family.

MAKING CAKES

With all baking recipes, there are some basic principles that apply and this is especially true of cake making:

- Start by reading the recipe all the way through.
- Measure all the ingredients accurately and do basic preparation, such as grating and chopping, before you start cooking.
- Basic cake-making ingredients should be kept at room temperature.
- Mixtures that are creamed together, a process which involves beating butter and sugar together, should be almost white and have a "soft dropping" consistency. This can be done by hand, but an electric mixer will save you time and effort.
- "Folding in" is achieved by using a metal spoon or spatula and working as gently as possible to fold through the flour or dry ingredients in a figure-eight movement.
- Do not remove a cake from the oven until it is fully cooked. To test if a cake is cooked, press the surface lightly with your fingertips—it should feel springy to the touch. Alternatively, insert a toothpick into the center of the cake—it will come out clean if the cake is cooked through.
- Leave cakes in their pans to cool before carefully turning out onto a wire rack to cool completely.

MAKING PIES & TARTS

When making the pies or tarts in the book, follow these basic principles:

- Sift the dry ingredients into a large mixing bowl, add the diced butter, and toss it through the flour.
- Gently rub the butter between your fingertips, a little at a time, until the mixture looks like fine breadcrumbs and, as you rub in the mixture, lift your hands up to aerate the mixture as it falls back into the bowl.
- Bind the mixture with iced water or other liquid, using just enough to make a soft dough. Wrap the dough and chill for at least 30 minutes.

Puddings
& Pastries

No meal is really complete without a dessert, and this chapter indulges the reader with a hearty and wholesome collection of some best-loved recipes. Fruit puddings, chocolate puddings, lemon puddings, and crumbly puddings—they are all fun, easy to make, and delicious. This chapter also offers some new surprises for old-fashioned puddings, leaving you with the difficult decision of which to try first; will it be Plum Cobbler or Mini Frangipane Tarts with Lime?

Soft, crumbly, and melt-in-your-mouth pastry holds the secret to success with a wide variety of magnificent dishes. Pie dough is used in several recipes in this chapter, and it is important to remember that a light touch when preparing the dough will give a much better result.

Where "fresh ready-made pie dough" and "fresh ready-made puff pastry" is specified in the recipes, the quality that you get from the supermarket products is extremely good and saves you time on certain recipes.

Eve's Pudding

Serves 6

INGREDIENTS

1 pound cooking apples,
  peeled, cored, and sliced
$^1/_3$ cup granulated sugar
1 tbsp lemon juice
$^1/_3$ cup golden raisins
$^1/_3$ cup butter
$^1/_3$ cup superfine sugar

1 egg, beaten
1$^1/_4$ cups self-rising flour
3 tbsp milk

$^1/_4$ cup slivered almonds
custard or heavy cream,
  to serve

1 Thoroughly grease a 3½ cup ovenproof dish.

2 Mix the apples with the sugar, lemon juice, and golden raisins. Spoon the mixture into the dish.

3 In a bowl, cream the butter and superfine sugar together until pale. Add the egg, a little at a time.

4 Carefully fold in the self-rising flour and stir in the milk to give a soft, dropping consistency.

5 Spread the mixture over the apples and sprinkle with the slivered almonds.

6 Bake in a preheated oven at 350°F for 40–45 minutes, until the sponge is a light golden brown color.

7 Serve the pudding hot, with custard or heavy cream.

COOK'S TIP

To increase the almond flavor of this apple pudding, add ¼ cup ground almonds with the flour in step 4.

Queen of Puddings

Serves 8

INGREDIENTS

2 1/2 cups milk
2 tbsp butter
1 1/4 cups superfine sugar
finely grated rind of 1 orange

4 eggs, separated
3/4 cup fresh breadcrumbs

pinch of salt
6 tbsp orange marmalade

1 Thoroughly grease a 6 cup ovenproof dish.

2 To make the custard, heat the milk in a pan with the butter, 1/4 cup of the superfine sugar, and the grated orange rind until just warm.

3 Whisk the egg yolks in a bowl. Gradually pour the warm milk over the eggs, stirring.

4 Stir the breadcrumbs into the pan, then transfer the mixture to the prepared dish, and let stand for 15 minutes.

5 Bake in a preheated oven at 350°F for 20–25 minutes, until the custard has just set. Remove the custard from the oven, but do not turn the oven off.

6 To make the meringue, whisk the egg whites with a pinch of salt until they stand in soft peaks. Whisk in the remaining sugar, a little at a time.

7 Spread the orange marmalade over the cooked custard. Top with the meringue, spreading it to the edges of the dish.

8 Return the pudding to the oven and bake for a further 20 minutes, until the meringue is crisp and golden.

Bread & Butter Pudding

Serves 6

INGREDIENTS

7 ounces white bread, sliced
4 tbsp butter, softened
2 tbsp golden raisins
1/8 cup candied peel
2 1/2 cups milk

4 egg yolks
1/3 cup superfine sugar
1/2 tsp apple pie spice

1 Grease a 5 1/3 cup ovenproof dish.

2 Remove the crusts from the bread (optional). Spread with the butter and cut the slices in half.

3 Arrange half of the buttered bread slices in the prepared ovenproof dish. Sprinkle half of the golden raisins and candied peel over the top of the bread.

4 Place the remaining bread slices over the fruit, and then top with the reserved fruit.

5 To make the custard, bring the milk almost to a boil in a saucepan. Whisk together the egg yolks and the sugar in a bowl, then pour in the warm milk.

6 Pour the warm custard through a strainer. Then pour the custard over the bread slices.

7 Let stand for 30 minutes, then sprinkle with the apple pie spice.

8 Place the ovenproof dish in a roasting pan half-filled with hot water.

9 Bake in a preheated oven at 400°F for 40–45 minutes, until the pudding has just set. Serve warm.

Plum Cobbler

Serves 6

INGREDIENTS

2¼ pounds plums, pits removed, and sliced
⅓ cup superfine sugar
1 tbsp lemon juice
2¼ cups all-purpose flour
⅓ cup granulated sugar

2 tsp baking powder
1 egg, beaten
⅔ cup buttermilk

6 tbsp butter, melted and cooled
heavy cream, to serve

1 Lightly grease an 8 cup ovenproof dish.

2 In a large bowl, mix together the plums, superfine sugar, lemon juice, and ¼ cup of the all-purpose flour.

3 Spoon the coated plums into the bottom of the ovenproof dish.

4 Mix together the remaining flour, granulated sugar, and baking powder in a bowl until well combined.

5 Add the beaten egg, buttermilk, and cooled melted butter. Mix together to form a soft dough.

6 Place spoonfuls of the dough on top of the fruit mixture until it is almost covered.

7 Bake the cobbler in a preheated oven at 375°F for about 35–40 minutes, until golden brown and bubbling.

8 Serve the pudding hot, with heavy cream.

COOK'S TIP

If you cannot find buttermilk, try using sour cream.

Blackberry Pudding

Serves 4

INGREDIENTS

1 pound blackberries
$^1/_3$ cup superfine sugar
1 egg
$^1/_3$ cup light brown sugar

6 tbsp butter, melted
8 tbsp milk
1 cup self-rising flour

1 Lightly grease a large 3½ cup ovenproof dish.

2 In a large mixing bowl, gently mix together the blackberries and superfine sugar until they are thoroughly combined.

3 Transfer the blackberry and sugar mixture to the prepared ovenproof dish.

4 Beat together the egg and light brown sugar in a mixing bowl until well combined. Stir in the melted butter and milk.

5 Sift the flour into the egg and butter mixture and fold together lightly to form a smooth batter.

6 Carefully spread the batter over the blackberry and sugar mixture in the dish, to cover the fruit.

7 Bake the pudding in a preheated oven at 350°F for 25–30 minutes, until the topping is firm and golden.

8 Sprinkle the pudding with a little sugar, if desired, and serve hot.

VARIATION

You can add 2 tablespoons of unsweetened cocoa to the batter in step 5, if you prefer a chocolate flavor.

Raspberry Shortcake

Serves 8

INGREDIENTS

1¹/₂ cups self-rising flour
7 tbsp butter, cut into cubes
¹/₃ cup superfine sugar

1 egg yolk
1 tbsp rose water
2¹/₂ cups whipping cream,
  whipped lightly
1¹/₃ cups raspberries, plus a
  few for decoration

TO DECORATE:
confectioners' sugar
mint leaves

1 Lightly grease 2 cookie sheets.

2 To make the shortcakes, sift the flour into a bowl.

3 Rub the butter into the flour with your fingers until the mixture resembles breadcrumbs.

4 Stir the sugar, egg yolk, and rose water into the mixture and bring together with your fingertips to form a soft dough. Divide the dough in half.

5 Roll each piece of dough to an 8-inch round and place each one onto a prepared cookie sheet. Crimp the edges of the dough.

6 Bake in a preheated oven at 375°F for 15 minutes, until lightly golden. Transfer the shortcakes to a wire rack and let cool.

7 Mix the cream with the raspberries and spoon on top of one of the shortcake rounds. Top with the other shortcake round, dust with a little confectioners' sugar, and decorate with the extra raspberries and mint leaves.

COOK'S TIP

The shortcake can be made a few days in advance and stored in an airtight container until required.

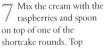

Pavlova

Serves 6

INGREDIENTS

3 egg whites
pinch of salt
³/₄ cup superfine sugar

1¹/₄ cups heavy cream, lightly
   whipped

fresh fruit of your choice
   (raspberries, strawberries,
   peaches, passion fruit,
   ground cherries)

1 Line a large cookie sheet with a sheet of baking parchment.

2 Whisk the egg whites with the salt in a bowl until they form soft peaks.

3 Whisk in the sugar a little at a time, whisking well after each addition.

4 Spoon three-quarters of the meringue onto the cookie sheet, forming a round 8 inches in diameter.

5 Place spoonfuls of the remaining meringue all around the edge of the round so they join up to make a nest shape.

6 Bake in a preheated oven at 275°F for 1¹/₄ hours.

7 Turn the heat off, but leave the pavlova in the oven until it is completely cold.

8 To serve, transfer the pavlova to a serving dish. Gently spread with the lightly whipped heavy cream, then arrange the fresh fruit on top.

COOK'S TIP

It is a good idea to make the pavlova in the evening and leave it in the turned-off oven overnight.

Sticky Chocolate Pudding

Serves 6

INGREDIENTS

$^1/_2$ cup butter, softened
$^3/_4$ cup light brown sugar
3 eggs, beaten

pinch of salt
$^1/_4$ cup unsweetened cocoa
1 cup self-rising flour
1 ounce dark chocolate,
    finely chopped
$2^3/_4$ ounces white chocolate,
    finely chopped

SAUCE:
$^2/_3$ cup heavy cream
$^1/_3$ cup light brown sugar
2 tbsp butter

1 Lightly grease 6 individual $^3/_4$ cup pudding molds.

2 Cream together the butter and sugar until pale and fluffy. Beat in the eggs, a little at a time.

3 Sift the salt, unsweetened cocoa, and flour into the creamed mixture and fold through the mixture. Stir the chopped chocolate into the mixture until evenly combined.

4 Divide the mixture between the prepared pudding molds. Lightly grease 6 squares of foil and use them to cover the tops of the molds. Press around the edges to seal.

5 Place the molds in a roasting pan and pour in boiling water to come halfway up the sides of the molds.

6 Bake in a preheated oven at 350°F for 50 minutes, or until a toothpick

inserted into the center comes out clean. Remove the molds from the roasting pan and set aside.

7 To make the sauce, put the cream, sugar, and butter into a pan and bring to a boil over a gentle heat. Simmer gently until the sugar has dissolved.

8 Turn the puddings out onto individual serving plates. Pour the sauce over the top of the puddings and serve.

Chocolate Brownie Roulade

Serves 8

INGREDIENTS

5¹/₂ ounces dark chocolate,
    broken into pieces
3 tbsp water
³/₄ cup superfine sugar
5 eggs, separated

2 tbsp raisins, chopped
¹/₄ cup chopped pecans
pinch of salt

1¹/₄ cups heavy cream,
    whipped lightly
confectioners' sugar, for
    dusting

1 Grease a 12 × 8-inch jelly roll pan and line with greased baking parchment.

2 Heat the chocolate with the water in a small saucepan over a low heat until the chocolate has just melted. Let cool.

3 Whisk the sugar and egg yolks for about 2–3 minutes until thick. Fold in the chocolate, raisins, and pecans.

4 Whisk the egg whites with the salt. Fold one-quarter of the egg whites into the chocolate mixture, then lightly fold in the rest.

5 Transfer the mixture to the prepared pan and bake in a preheated oven at 350°F for 25 minutes, until risen and just firm to the touch. Remove from the oven and let cool before covering with a sheet of nonstick baking parchment and a damp clean dish cloth. Leave until completely cold.

6 Turn the roulade out onto another piece of baking parchment dusted with confectioners' sugar and remove the lining paper.

7 Spread the whipped heavy cream over the roulade. Starting from a short end, roll the sponge away from you using the paper to guide you. Trim the ends of the roulade to make a neat finish and transfer to a serving plate. Chill in the refrigerator until ready to serve. Dust with a little confectioners' sugar before serving, if desired.

One Roll Fruit Pie

Serves 8

INGREDIENTS

PIE DOUGH:
1$\frac{1}{2}$ cups all-purpose flour
7 tbsp butter, cut into
    small pieces
1 tbsp water
1 egg, separated

sugar cubes, crushed, for
    sprinkling

FILLING:
1$\frac{1}{2}$ pound prepared fruit
    (rhubarb, gooseberries,
    plums, damsons)

6 tbsp light brown sugar
1 tbsp ground ginger

1 Thoroughly grease a large cookie sheet with a little butter.

2 To make the pie dough, place the flour and butter in a mixing bowl and rub in the butter with your fingers. Add the water and work the mixture together until a soft pie dough has formed. Wrap and chill for 30 minutes.

3 Roll out the chilled pie dough to a round measuring about 14 inches in diameter.

4 Transfer the round to the center of the greased cookie sheet. Brush the pie dough with the egg yolk.

5 To make the filling, mix the prepared fruit with the brown sugar and ground ginger and pile it into the center of the pie dough.

6 Turn in the edges of the pie dough all the way around. Brush the surface of the pie dough with the egg white and sprinkle evenly with the crushed sugar cubes.

7 Bake in a preheated oven at 400°F for 35 minutes, or until golden brown. Serve warm.

Fruit Crumble Tart

Serves 8

INGREDIENTS

PIE DOUGH:
1¼ cups all-purpose flour
5 tsp superfine sugar
9 tbsp butter, cut into small
    pieces
1 tbsp water

FILLING:
1½ cups raspberries
1 pound plums, halved, pitted,
    and roughly chopped
3 tbsp raw crystal sugar

TO SERVE:
light cream

TOPPING:
1 cup all-purpose flour
⅓ cup raw crystal sugar
⅓ cup butter, cut into small
    pieces
1 cup chopped mixed nuts
1 tsp ground cinnamon

1 To make the pie dough, place the flour, sugar, and butter in a bowl and rub in the butter with your fingers. Add the water and work the mixture together until a soft pie dough has formed. Wrap and chill for 30 minutes.

2 Roll out the pie dough to line the base of a 10-inch loose-bottomed quiche pan. Prick the base of the pie dough with a fork and chill for about 30 minutes.

3 To make the filling, toss the raspberries and plums together with the sugar and spoon into the pie shell.

4 To make the crumble topping, combine the flour, sugar, and butter in a bowl. Work the butter into the flour with your fingers until the mixture resembles coarse breadcrumbs. Stir in the nuts and ground cinnamon.

5 Sprinkle the topping over the fruit and bake in a preheated oven at 400°F for 20–25 minutes, until the topping is golden. Serve with light cream.

Cheese & Apple Tart

Serves 8

INGREDIENTS

1¹/₂ cups self-rising flour
1 tsp baking powder
pinch of salt

¹/₃ cup light brown sugar
³/₄ cup pitted dates, chopped
1 pound 2 ounces eating
    apples, cored and chopped
¹/₂ cup chopped walnuts
¹/₄ cup sunflower oil

2 eggs
1¹/₂ cups grated Red Leicester
    cheese

1 Grease a 10-inch loose-bottomed quiche pan with butter and line with baking parchment.

2 Sift the flour, baking powder, and salt into a bowl. Stir in the brown sugar and the chopped dates, apples, and walnuts. Thoroughly mix together until well combined.

3 Beat the oil and eggs together and add the mixture to the dry ingredients. Stir until thoroughly combined.

4 Spoon half of the mixture into the pan and level the surface.

5 Sprinkle with the cheese, then spoon over the remaining cake mixture, spreading it to the edges of the pan.

6 Bake in a preheated oven at 350°F for 45–50 minutes, or until golden brown and firm to the touch.

7 Cool slightly in the pan. Serve warm.

COOK'S TIP

This is a deliciously moist tart. Any leftovers should be stored in the refrigerator and heated to serve.

Apple Tart Tatin

Serves 8

INGREDIENTS

9 tbsp butter
$^1/_2$ cup superfine sugar
4 eating apples, cored and
quartered

9 ounces fresh ready-made
pie dough
crème fraîche, to serve

1 Heat the butter and sugar in a 9-inch ovenproof skillet over a medium heat for about 5 minutes, until the mixture begins to caramelize. Remove the skillet from the heat.

2 Arrange the apple quarters, skin side down, in the skillet, taking care as the butter and sugar are very hot. Place the skillet back on the heat and simmer for 2 minutes.

3 On a lightly floured surface, roll out the pie dough to form a round just larger than the skillet.

4 Place the pie dough over the apples, press down, and tuck in the edges to seal the apples under the layer of pie dough.

5 Bake in a preheated oven at 400°F for 20–25 minutes, until the pie dough is golden. Remove from the oven and let cool for 10 minutes.

6 Place a serving plate over the skillet and invert so that the pastry forms the base of the turned-out tart. Serve the tart warm with crème fraîche.

VARIATION

Replace the apples with pears, if you prefer. Leave the skin on the pears, cut them into quarters, and then remove the cores.

Syrup Tart

Serves 8

INGREDIENTS

9 ounces fresh ready-made
   shortcrust pie dough
1 cup light corn syrup
2 cups fresh white
   breadcrumbs
$^1/_2$ cup heavy cream

finely grated rind of $^1/_2$ lemon
   or orange
2 tbsp lemon or orange juice
custard, to serve

1 Roll out the pie dough to line an 8-inch loose-bottomed quiche pan, reserving the pie dough trimmings. Prick the base of the pie dough with a fork and chill in the refrigerator.

2 Cut out small shapes from the reserved pie dough trimmings, such as leaves, stars, or hearts, to decorate the top of the syrup tart.

3 In a mixing bowl, mix together the corn syrup, breadcrumbs, cream, grated lemon or orange rind, and lemon or orange juice.

4 Pour the mixture into the pie shell and decorate the edges of the tart with the pie dough cut-outs.

5 Bake in a preheated oven at 375°F for 35–40 minutes, or until the filling is just set.

6 Leave the tart to cool slightly in the pan for about 10–15 minutes, then turn out and serve the tart accompanied by custard.

VARIATION

Use the pie dough trimmings to create a lattice pattern on top of the tart, if preferred.

Apple & Mincemeat Tart

Serves 8

INGREDIENTS

PIE DOUGH:
1¼ cups all-purpose flour
2 tbsp superfine sugar
½ cup butter, cut into
    small pieces
1 tbsp water

FILLING:
14½ ounce jar mincemeat
3 eating apples, cored
1 tbsp lemon juice
6 tsp light corn syrup
3 tbsp butter

1 To make the pie dough, place the flour and superfine sugar in a large mixing bowl, add the butter, and rub in with your fingertips until the mixture resembles fine breadcrumbs.

2 Add the water and work the mixture together until a soft pie dough has formed. Wrap and chill in the refrigerator for 30 minutes.

3 On a lightly floured surface, roll out the dough and line a 10-inch loose-bottomed quiche pan. Prick the dough with a fork and chill in the refrigerator for 30 minutes.

4 Line the pie shell with foil and dried beans. Bake the shell in a preheated oven at 375°F for 15 minutes. Remove the foil and beans and cook the shell for another 15 minutes.

5 Grate the apple and mix with the mincemeat and lemon juice until well combined and spoon into the baked pie shell.

6 Melt the syrup and butter together and pour over the mincemeat mixture.

7 Return the tart to the oven for 20 minutes, until firm. Serve warm.

VARIATION

Add 2 tbsp sherry to spice up the mincemeat, if you wish.

Custard Tart

Serves 8

INGREDIENTS

PIE DOUGH;
1 1/4 cups all-purpose flour
5 tsp superfine sugar
1/2 cup butter, cut into small
  pieces
1 tbsp water

FILLING:
3 eggs
2/3 cup light cream
2/3 cup milk
freshly grated nutmeg

TO SERVE:
whipped cream

1 To make the pie dough, place the flour and sugar in a mixing bowl and rub in the butter with your fingertips until the mixture resembles fine breadcrumbs.

2 Add the water and mix together until a soft pie dough has formed. Wrap and chill in the refrigerator for about 30 minutes.

3 Roll out the dough to form a round slightly larger than a 10-inch loose-bottomed quiche pan.

4 Line the pan with the dough, trimming off the edges. Prick the dough with a fork and chill in the refrigerator for 30 minutes.

5 Line the pie shell with a sheet of foil and dried beans.

6 Bake in a preheated oven at 375°F for 15 minutes. Remove the foil and beans and bake the pie shell for a further 15 minutes.

7 To make the filling, whisk together the eggs, cream, milk, and nutmeg. Pour the filling into the prepared pie shell. Transfer the tart to the oven and cook for about 25–30 minutes, or until just set. Serve with whipped cream, if desired.

Lemon Tart

Serves 8

INGREDIENTS

PIE DOUGH:
1 1/4 cups all-purpose flour
5 tsp superfine sugar
1/2 cup butter, cut into small
   pieces
1 tbsp water

FILLING:
2/3 cup heavy cream
1/2 cup superfine sugar
4 eggs
grated rind of 3 lemons
12 tbsp lemon juice

confectioners' sugar, for
   dusting

1 To make the pie dough, place the flour and sugar in a bowl and rub in the butter using your fingertips. Add the water and mix until a soft pie dough has formed. Wrap and chill for 30 minutes.

2 On a lightly floured surface, roll out the dough and line a 10-inch loose-bottomed quiche pan. Prick the pie dough all over with a fork and chill for 30 minutes.

3 Line the pie shell with foil and dried beans and bake blind in a preheated oven at 375°F for 15 minutes. Remove the foil and beans, return to the oven and cook the pie shell for another 15 minutes.

4 To make the filling, whisk the cream, sugar, eggs, and lemon rind and juice together. Place the pie shell, still in its pan, on a cookie sheet and pour in the filling.

5 Bake in the oven for about 20 minutes, or until just set. Let to cool, then lightly dust with confectioners' sugar before serving.

Orange Tart

Serves 6–8

INGREDIENTS

PIE DOUGH:
1¼ cups all-purpose flour
5 tsp superfine sugar
½ cup butter, cut into
    small pieces
1 tbsp water

FILLING:
grated rind of 2 oranges
9 tbsp orange juice
⅞ cups fresh white
    breadcrumbs
2 tbsp lemon juice
⅔ cup light cream
¼ cup butter

¼ cup superfine sugar
2 eggs, separated
pinch of salt

1 To make the pie dough, place the flour and sugar in a large bowl and rub in the butter. Add the cold water and work the mixture together until a soft pie dough has formed. Wrap and leave to chill for 30 minutes.

2 Roll out the dough and line a 10-inch loose-bottomed quiche pan. Prick the pie dough with a fork and chill for 30 minutes.

3 Line the pie shell with foil and dried beans and bake in a preheated oven at 375°F for 15 minutes. Remove the foil and beans and cook the pie shell for a further 15 minutes.

4 To make the filling, mix the orange rind, orange juice and breadcrumbs in a bowl. Stir in the lemon juice and light cream. Melt the butter and sugar over a low heat. Remove the pan from the heat, add the 2 egg

yolks, the salt, and the breadcrumb mixture and stir to combine.

5 Whisk the egg whites with the salt until they form soft peaks. Fold them into the egg yolk mixture.

6 Pour the filling mixture into the pie shell. Bake in a preheated oven at 325°F for about 45 minutes, or until just set. Cool slightly and serve warm.

Coconut Cream Tart

Serves 6–8

INGREDIENTS

PIE DOUGH:

1¹/4 cups all-purpose flour

5 tsp superfine sugar

¹/2 cup butter, cut into
small pieces

1 tbsp water

FILLING:

2 cups milk

4¹/2 ounces creamed coconut

3 egg yolks

¹/2 cup superfine sugar

¹/2 cup all-purpose flour,
sifted

¹/3 cup shredded coconut

¹/4 cup chopped candied
pineapple

2 tbsp rum or pineapple juice

1¹/4 cups whipping cream,
whipped

1 To make the pie dough, place the flour and sugar in a bowl and rub in the butter. Add the water and work the mixture together until a soft pie dough has formed. Wrap and chill for 30 minutes.

2 On a lightly floured surface, roll out the dough and line a 10-inch loose-bottomed quiche pan. Prick the pie dough with a fork and chill for

30 minutes. Line the pie shell with foil and dried beans and bake in a preheated oven at 375°F for 15 minutes. Remove the foil and beans and cook the pie shell for a further 15 minutes. Let cool.

3 To make the filling, bring the milk and creamed coconut to just below boiling point in a pan, stirring to melt the coconut.

4 Whisk the egg yolks with the sugar until fluffy. Whisk in the flour. Add the hot milk, stirring. Return the mixture to the pan and gently heat for 8 minutes, until thick, stirring. Let cool.

5 Stir in the coconut, pineapple, rum or pineapple juice, and spread the filling in the pie shell. Cover with the whipped cream and chill.

Pine Nut Tart

Serves 8

INGREDIENTS

PIE DOUGH:
1¼ cups all-purpose flour
5 tsp superfine sugar
½ cup butter, cut into
    small pieces
1 tbsp water

FILLING:
1¼ cups cottage cheese
4 tbsp heavy cream
3 eggs
½ cup superfine sugar
grated rind of 1 orange
1 cup pine nuts

1 To make the pie dough, place the flour and sugar in a bowl and rub in the butter with your fingertips. Add the water and work the mixture together until a soft pie dough has formed. Wrap and chill for 30 minutes.

2 On a lightly floured surface, roll out the dough and line a 10-inch loose-bottomed quiche pan. Prick the pie dough all over with a fork and chill for 30 minutes.

3 Line the pie shell with foil and dried beans and bake in a preheated oven at 375°F for 15 minutes. Remove the foil and beans and cook the pie shell for a further 15 minutes.

4 To make the filling, beat together the curd cheese, cream, eggs, sugar, orange rind, and half of the pine nuts. Pour the filling into the prepared pie shell and sprinkle with the remaining pine nuts.

5 Bake in the oven at 325°F for 35 minutes, or until just set. Set aside and cool slightly before serving.

Candied Peel & Nut Tart

Serves 8

INGREDIENTS

PIE DOUGH:
1¼ cups all-purpose flour
5 tsp superfine sugar
½ cup butter, cut into
    small pieces
1 tbsp water

FILLING:
6 tbsp butter
¼ cup superfine sugar
⅓ cup set honey
¾ cup heavy cream
1 egg, beaten
1¾ cups mixed nuts

⅞ cup candied peel

1 To make the pie dough, place the flour and sugar in a bowl and rub in the pieces of butter with your fingertips. Add the water and work the mixture together to form a soft pie dough. Wrap and chill for 30 minutes.

2 On a lightly floured surface, roll out the dough and line a 10-inch loose-bottomed quiche pan. Prick the pie dough all over with a fork and chill for 30 minutes.

3 Line the pie shell with foil and dried beans and bake in a preheated oven at 375°F for 15 minutes. Remove the foil and beans and cook for 15 minutes longer.

4 To make the filling, melt the butter, sugar, and honey in a pan. Stir in the cream and beaten egg, then add the nuts and candied peel. Cook over a low heat, stirring, for 2 minutes, until the mixture is a pale golden color.

5 Pour the filling into the pie shell and bake for 15–20 minutes, or until just set. Let cool, then serve in slices.

Apricot & Cranberry Frangipane Tart

Serves 8–10

INGREDIENTS

PIE DOUGH:
1¹/₄ cups all-purpose flour
¹/₂ cup superfine sugar
¹/₂ cup butter, cut into
small pieces
1 tbsp water

FILLING:
⁷/₈ cup sweet butter
1 cup superfine sugar
1 egg
2 egg yolks
¹/₃ cup all-purpose flour,
sifted
1¹/₂ cups ground almonds
4 tbsp heavy cream

14¹/₂ ounce can apricot
halves, drained
1 cup fresh cranberries

1 Place the flour and sugar in a bowl and rub in the butter. Add the water and work the mixture together until a soft pie dough has formed. Wrap and chill for 30 minutes.

2 Roll out the dough and line a 10-inch loose-bottomed quiche pan. Prick the dough with a fork and chill for 30 minutes.

3 Line the pie shell with foil and dried beans and bake in a preheated oven at 375°F for 15 minutes. Remove the foil and beans, return the pie shell to the oven and cook for a further 10 minutes.

4 To make the filling, cream together the butter and sugar until light and fluffy. Beat in the egg and egg yolks, then stir in the flour, almonds, and cream.

5 Place the apricot halves and cranberries on the bottom of the pie shell and spoon the filling over the top.

6 Bake in the oven for about 1 hour, or until the topping is just set. Cool slightly, then serve warm or cold.

White Chocolate & Almond Tart

Serves 8

INGREDIENTS

PIE DOUGH:
1¼ cups all-purpose flour
5 tsp superfine sugar
½ cup butter, cut into
    small pieces
1 tbsp water

FILLING:
¾ cup light corn syrup
2 tbsp butter
⅓ cup light brown sugar
3 eggs, lightly beaten
½ cup whole blanched
    almonds, roughly chopped

3½ ounces white chocolate,
    roughly chopped
cream, to serve (optional)

1 To make the pie shell, place the flour and sugar in a mixing bowl and rub in the butter with your fingers. Add the water and work the mixture together until a soft pie dough has formed. Wrap and chill for 30 minutes.

2 On a lightly floured surface, roll out the dough and line a 10-inch loose-bottomed quiche pan. Prick the pie dough all over with a fork and chill for 30 minutes. Line the pie shell with foil and dried beans and bake in a preheated oven at 375°F for 15 minutes. Remove the foil and beans, return the pie shell to the oven and cook for a further 15 minutes.

3 To make the filling, gently melt the syrup, butter, and sugar together in a saucepan. Remove from the heat and let cool slightly. Add the beaten eggs, almonds, and chocolate, and stir until well blended.

4 Pour the chocolate and nut filling into the prepared pie shell and cook in the oven for 30–35 minutes, or until just set. Let cool before removing from the pan. Serve with cream, if desired.

Mincemeat & Grape Jalousie

Serves 4

INGREDIENTS

1 pound 2 ounces fresh ready-made puff pastry	3¹/₂ ounces grapes, seeded and halved	raw crystal sugar, for sprinkling
14¹/₂ ounce jar mincemeat	1 egg, for glazing	

1 Lightly grease a cookie sheet with a little butter.

2 On a lightly floured surface, roll out the dough and cut it into 2 rectangles.

3 Place one dough rectangle onto the prepared cookie sheet and brush the edges with water.

4 Combine the mincemeat and grapes in a mixing bowl. Spread the mixture over the dough rectangle on the cookie sheet, leaving a 1-inch border all around.

5 Fold the second dough rectangle in half lengthwise. Using a sharp knife, carefully cut a series of parallel lines across the folded edge, leaving a 1-inch border.

6 Open out the puff pastry dough rectangle and lay it over the mincemeat. Seal down the edges of the dough and press together well.

7 Flute and crimp the edges of the dough. Lightly brush the dough with the beaten egg and sprinkle with a little raw crystal sugar.

8 Bake the jalousie in a preheated oven at 425°F for about 15 minutes. Lower the heat to 350°F and cook for a further 30 minutes, until the jalousie is well risen and golden brown. Cool on a wire rack before serving.

COOK'S TIP

For an enhanced festive flavor, stir 2 tbsp sherry into the mincemeat.

Pear Tarts

Makes 6

INGREDIENTS

9 ounces fresh ready-made puff pastry

8 tsp light brown sugar

2 tbsp butter (plus extra for brushing)

1 tbsp finely chopped preserved ginger

3 pears, peeled, halved, and cored

cream, to serve

1 On a lightly floured surface, roll out the dough. Cut out six rounds 4 inches in diameter

2 Place the rounds on a large cookie sheet and chill in the refrigerator for 30 minutes.

3 Cream together the brown sugar and butter in a small bowl, then stir in the chopped preserved ginger.

4 Prick the pastry rounds all over with a fork and spread a little of the ginger mixture onto each one.

5 Slice the pears halves lengthwise, keeping the pears intact at the tip. Carefully fan out the slices slightly.

6 Place a fanned-out pear half on top of each dough round. Make small flutes around the edge of the dough rounds and generously brush each pear half with melted butter.

7 Bake in a preheated oven at 400°F for 15–20 minutes, until the pastry is well risen and golden in color. Serve warm with a little cream.

COOK'S TIP

If you prefer, serve these tarts with vanilla ice cream for a delicious dessert.

Crème Brûlée Tarts

Makes 6

INGREDIENTS

PIE DOUGH:
1$\frac{1}{4}$ cups all-purpose flour
5 tsp superfine sugar
$\frac{1}{2}$ cup butter, cut into
    small pieces.
1 tbsp water

FILLING:
4 egg yolks
$\frac{1}{4}$ cup superfine sugar
1$\frac{3}{4}$ cups heavy cream
1 tsp vanilla extract
raw crystal sugar,
    for sprinkling

1 Place the flour and sugar in a large mixing bowl and rub in the butter. Add the water and work the mixture together until a soft pie dough has formed. Wrap and chill for 30 minutes.

2 Roll out the dough to line six 4-inch tart pans. Prick the bottom of the pie dough all over with a fork and chill in the refrigerator for 20 minutes.

3 Line the pie shells with foil and dried beans and bake in a preheated oven at 375°F for 15 minutes. Remove the foil and beans and cook the pie shells for a further 10 minutes, until crisp and golden. Let cool.

4 Meanwhile, make the filling. In a bowl, beat the egg yolks and sugar until pale. Heat the cream and vanilla extract in a pan until just below boiling point, then pour it onto the egg mixture, whisking constantly.

5 Place the mixture in a pan and bring to just below a boil, stirring, until thick. Do not allow to boil or it will curdle.

6 Let the mixture cool slightly, then pour it into the tart pans. Cool and then chill overnight.

7 Sprinkle the tarts with the sugar. Place under a preheated broiler for a few minutes. Cool, then chill for 2 hours before serving.

Mini Frangipane Tarts with Lime

Makes 12

INGREDIENTS

1 cup all-purpose flour
$^1/_3$ cup butter, softened
1 tsp grated lime rind
1 tbsp lime juice
4 tbsp superfine sugar
1 egg

$^1/_4$ cup ground almonds
$^1/_3$ cup confectioners' sugar, sifted
$^1/_2$ tbsp water

1 Reserve 5 teaspoons of the flour and 1 tablespoon of the butter and set aside until required.

2 Rub the remaining butter into the remaining flour, until the mixture resembles fine breadcrumbs. Stir in the lime rind, followed by the lime juice and bring the mixture together to form a soft dough.

3 On a lightly floured surface, roll out the dough thinly. Stamp out twelve 3-inch rounds and line a muffin pan.

4 In a bowl, cream together the reserved butter with the superfine sugar.

5 Mix in the egg, then the ground almonds and the reserved flour.

6 Divide the mixture between the pie shells.

7 Bake in a preheated oven at 400°F for 15 minutes, until set and lightly golden. Remove the tartlets from the pan and let cool.

8 Mix the confectioners' sugar with the water. Drizzle a little of the frosting over each tartlet and serve.

Breads & Side Dishes

Freshly baked bread has never been easier to make, especially with the easy blend yeasts available nowadays. In this chapter, packets containing 2 teaspoons of active dry yeast have been used, as it is easy to obtain, simple to use, and gives good results. If you want to use fresh yeast, replace one sachet of active dry yeast with 1 ounce of fresh yeast. Blend the fresh yeast into the warm liquid and add 1 teaspoon of sugar. Add to the flour and continue as usual.

Always choose a strong white or brown flour for the bread recipes using yeast, it contains a high proportion of gluten, the protein which gives the dough its elasticity. Always knead the dough thoroughly—this can be done in an electric mixer with the dough hook attachment for about 5–8 minutes, but kneading by hand is most enjoyable and satisfying.

This chapter also has a selection of side dishes to savor, including tasty pies, pastries, and flans to create a whole medley of delicious dishes that can be used as part of a main meal.

Teacakes

Serves 12

INGREDIENTS

4 cups strong white
    bread flour
1 packet active dry yeast
3 tbsp superfine sugar
1 tsp salt

2 tbsp butter, cut into
    small pieces
1¼ cups lukewarm milk
½ cup luxury dried fruit mix
honey, for brushing

1 Thoroughly grease several cookie sheets.

2 Sift the flour into a large mixing bowl. Stir in the yeast, sugar, and salt. Rub in the butter with your fingers until the mixture resembles fine breadcrumbs. Add the milk and mix all of the ingredients together to form a soft dough.

3 Place the dough on a lightly floured surface and knead for about 5 minutes (alternatively, you can knead the dough with an electric mixer with a dough hook).

4 Place the dough in a greased bowl, cover, and let rise in a warm place for 1–1½ hours, until it has doubled in size.

5 Knead the dough again for a few minutes and knead in the fruit. Divide the dough into 12 rounds and place on the cookie sheets. Cover and leave for 1 hour longer, or until springy to the touch when pressed lightly with a finger.

6 Bake in a preheated oven at 400°F for 20 minutes. Brush the teacakes with honey while still warm.

7 Cool the teacakes on a wire rack before serving them split in half. Spread with butter and serve.

Cinnamon Swirls

Makes 12

INGREDIENTS

2 cups strong white
   bread flour
$1/2$ tsp salt
1 packet active dry yeast
2 tbsp butter, cut into
   small pieces
1 egg, beaten

$1/2$ cup warm milk
2 tbsp maple syrup

FILLING:
4 tbsp butter, softened
3 tbsp light brown sugar
2 tsp ground cinnamon
$1/3$ cup currants

1 Thoroughly grease a 9-inch square baking pan.

2 Sift the flour and salt into a mixing bowl. Stir in the yeast. Rub in the butter with your fingertips until the mixture resembles breadcrumbs. Add the egg and milk and mix everything to form a dough.

3 Place the dough in a greased bowl, cover, and leave in a warm place for about 40 minutes, or until doubled in size.

4 Knead the dough lightly for 1 minute to punch down, then roll out to a rectangle 12 × 9 inches.

5 To make the filling, cream together the butter, brown sugar, and cinnamon, until light and fluffy. Spread the filling over the dough, leaving a 1-inch border. Sprinkle the currants on top.

6 Roll up the dough like a jelly roll, from a long edge, and press to seal. Cut the roll into 12 slices. Place them in the pan, cover, and leave for 30 minutes.

7 Bake in a preheated oven at 375°F for 20–30 minutes, or until well risen. Brush with the syrup and cool slightly before serving.

Cinnamon & Currant Loaf

Makes a 2-pound loaf

INGREDIENTS

3 cups all-purpose flour
pinch of salt
1 tbsp baking powder
1 tbsp ground cinnamon

²/3 cup butter, cut
    into small pieces
³/4 cup light brown sugar
³/4 cup currants
finely grated rind of 1 orange

5–6 tbsp orange juice
6 tbsp milk
2 eggs, lightly beaten

1 Thoroughly grease a 2-pound loaf pan and line the base with baking parchment.

2 Sift the flour, salt, baking powder, and ground cinnamon into a bowl. Rub in the butter pieces with your fingertips until the mixture resembles coarse breadcrumbs.

3 Stir in the sugar, currants, and orange rind. Beat the orange juice, milk, and eggs together and add to the dry ingredients. Mix well.

4 Spoon the mixture into the prepared pan. Make a slight dip in the middle of the mixture to help it rise evenly.

5 Bake in a preheated oven at 350°F for about 1–1 hour 10 minutes, or until a toothpick inserted into the center of the loaf comes out clean.

6 Let the loaf cool before turning out of the pan. Transfer to a wire rack and cool completely before slicing and serving.

COOK'S TIP

Once you have added the liquid to the dry ingredients, work as quickly as possible because the baking powder is activated by the liquid.

Orange, Banana, & Cranberry Loaf

Serves 8–10

INGREDIENTS

1 1/2 cups self-rising flour
1/2 tsp baking powder
1 cup light brown sugar
2 bananas, mashed

1/4 cup chopped candied peel
1/4 cup chopped mixed nuts
1/2 cup dried cranberries
5–6 tbsp orange juice
2 eggs, beaten
2/3 cup sunflower oil

1/3 cup confectioners' sugar, sifted
grated rind of 1 orange

1 Thotoughly grease a 2-pound loaf pan and line the base with baking parchment.

2 Sift the flour and baking powder into a large mixing bowl. Stir in the sugar, bananas, chopped candied peel, chopped nuts, and cranberries.

3 Stir the orange juice, eggs, and oil together until well combined. Add the mixture to the dry ingredients and mix until well blended. Pour the mixture into the prepared loaf pan.

4 Bake in a preheated oven at 350°F for about 1 hour, until firm to the touch or until a toothpick inserted into the center of the loaf comes out clean.

5 Turn out the loaf and cool on a wire rack.

6 Mix the confectioners' sugar with a little water and drizzle the frosting over the loaf. Sprinkle the orange rind over the top. Let the frosting set before serving the loaf in slices.

COOK'S TIP

This tea bread will keep for a couple of days. Wrap it carefully and store in a cool, dry place.

Banana & Date Loaf

Serves 6–8

INGREDIENTS

2 cups self-rising flour
$^1/_3$ cup butter, cut into
    small pieces
$^1/_3$ cup superfine sugar
$^7/_8$ cup chopped, pitted dates

2 bananas, roughly mashed
2 eggs, lightly beaten
2 tbsp clear honey

1 Thoroughly grease a 2-pound loaf pan and line the base with baking parchment.

2 Sift the flour into a large mixing bowl.

3 Rub the butter into the flour with your fingertips until the mixture resembles fine breadcrumbs.

4 Stir the sugar, chopped dates, bananas, beaten eggs, and honey into the dry ingredients. Mix together to form a soft dropping consistency.

5 Spoon the mixture into the prepared loaf pan and level the surface with the back of a knife.

6 Bake in a preheated oven at 325°F for about 1 hour, or until golden and a toothpick inserted into the center comes out clean.

7 Let the loaf cool in the pan before turning out and transferring to a wire rack.

8 Serve the loaf warm or cold, cut into thick slices.

COOK'S TIP

This tea bread will keep for several days if stored in an airtight container and kept in a cool, dry place.

Crown Loaf

Makes 1 loaf

INGREDIENTS

2 cups strong white bread
   flour
$^{1}/_{2}$ tsp salt
1 packet active dry yeast
2 tbsp butter, cut into
   small pieces
$^{1}/_{2}$ cup lukewarm milk
1 egg, beaten

FILLING:
4 tbsp butter, softened
3 tbsp light brown sugar
$^{1}/_{4}$ cup chopped hazelnuts
2 tbsp chopped preserved
   ginger
$^{1}/_{4}$ cup candied peel
1 tbsp rum or brandy
$^{2}/_{3}$ cup confectioners' sugar

2 tbsp lemon juice

1 Grease a cookie sheet. Sift the flour and salt into a bowl. Stir in the yeast. Rub in the butter. Add the milk and egg and mix together to form a dough.

2 Place the dough in a greased bowl, cover, and leave in a warm place for 40 minutes, until doubled in size. Knead the dough lightly for 1 minute to punch down. Roll out to a rectangle 12 × 9 inches.

3 Cream together the butter and sugar until light and fluffy. Stir in the hazelnuts, ginger, candied peel, and rum. Spread the filling over the dough, leaving a 1-inch border.

4 Roll up the dough from the long edge, to form a sausage shape. Cut into 2-inch slices and place on the cookie sheet in a circle with the slices just touching. Cover and let the dough rise in a warm place for 30 minutes.

5 Bake in a preheated oven at 325°F for 20–30 minutes, or until golden. Meanwhile, mix the confectioners' sugar with enough lemon juice to form a thin frosting.

6 Let the loaf cool slightly before drizzling the whole circle with frosting.

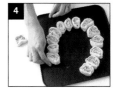

Date & Honey Loaf

Makes 1 loaf

INGREDIENTS

1¼ cups strong white bread
    flour
¼ cup strong brown bread
    flour
½ tsp salt

1 packet active dry yeast
¾ cup lukewarm water
3 tbsp sunflower oil

3 tbsp honey
½ cup chopped, pitted dates
2 tbsp sesame seeds

1 Grease a 2-pound loaf pan. Sift the white and brown flours into a large mixing bowl, stir in the salt and yeast.

2 Pour in the water, oil, and honey. Mix everything together to form a dough.

3 Place the dough on a lightly floured surface and knead for about 5 minutes, until smooth.

4 Place the dough in a greased bowl, cover, and let rise in a warm place for about 1 hour, or until doubled in size.

5 Knead in the dates and sesame seeds. Shape the dough and place in the pan.

6 Cover and leave in a warm place for another 30 minutes, or until springy to the touch.

7 Bake in a preheated oven at 425°F for 30 minutes, or until a hollow sound can be heard when the base of the loaf is tapped with the knuckles.

8 Transfer the loaf to a wire rack and let it cool. Serve the loaf, cut into thick slices.

VARIATION

Replace the sesame seeds with sunflower seeds for a slightly different texture, if you prefer.

COOK'S TIP

If you cannot find a warm place, sit the bowl over a saucepan of warm water.

Pumpkin Loaf

Serves 6–8

INGREDIENTS

3 1/2 cups chopped pumpkin
flesh
1/2 cup butter, softened
3/4 cup superfine sugar
2 eggs, beaten

2 cups all-purpose flour, sifted
1 1/2 tsp baking powder
1/2 tsp salt

1 tsp ground apple pie spice
1/3 cup pumpkin seeds

1 Grease a 2-pound loaf pan with oil.

2 Wrap the pumpkin pieces in buttered foil. Cook in a preheated oven at 400°F for about 30–40 minutes, until they are cooked through and tender.

3 Let the pumpkin cool completely before mashing well to make a thick purée.

4 In a bowl, cream the butter and sugar together until light and fluffy. Add the eggs, a little at a time.

5 Stir in the pumpkin purée. Fold in the flour, baking powder, salt, and apple pie spice.

6 Fold the pumpkin seeds through the mixture. Spoon the mixture into the prepared loaf pan.

7 Bake in a preheated oven at 325°F for about 1 1/4–1 1/2 hours, or until a toothpick inserted into the center of the loaf comes out clean.

8 Let the loaf cool and serve buttered, if desired.

COOK'S TIP

To ensure that the pumpkin purée is dry, place it in a saucepan over a medium heat for a few minutes, stirring frequently, until it is thick.

Tropical Fruit Bread

Makes 1 loaf

INGREDIENTS

3 cups strong white bread
   flour
5 tbsp bran
$^1/_2$ tsp salt
$^1/_2$ tsp ground ginger
1 packet active dry yeast
2 tbsp light brown sugar

2 tbsp butter, cut into
   small pieces
generous 1 cup lukewarm
   water
$^1/_2$ cup finely chopped,
   candied pineapple
3 tbsp finely chopped dried
   mango

$^2/_3$ cup shredded coconut,
   toasted
1 egg, beaten
2 tbsp coconut shreds

1 Thoroughly grease a cookie sheet. Sift the flour into a large mixing bowl. Stir in the bran, salt, ginger, yeast, and sugar. Rub in the butter with your fingers, then add the water, and mix to form a dough.

2 On a lightly floured surface, knead the dough for about 5–8 minutes, or until smooth (alternatively, use an electric mixer with a dough hook). Place the dough in a greased bowl, cover, and let rise in a warm place until doubled in size.

3 Knead the candied pineapple, dried mango, and shredded coconut into the dough. Shape into a round loaf and place on the cookie sheet. Score the top with the back of a knife. Cover and leave for a further 30 minutes in a warm place.

4 Brush the loaf with the egg and sprinkle with the 2 tbsp coconut. Bake in a preheated oven at 425°F for 30 minutes, or until golden in color.

5 Let the bread cool on a wire rack before serving.

Citrus Bread

Makes 1 loaf

INGREDIENTS

4 cups strong white bread flour	5–6 tbsp orange juice	2 tbsp clear honey
$^1/_2$ tsp salt	4 tbsp lemon juice	
$^1/_4$ cup superfine sugar	3–4 tbsp lime juice	
1 packet active dry yeast	$^2/_3$ cup lukewarm water	
4 tbsp butter, cut into small pieces	1 orange	
	1 lemon	
	1 lime	

1 Lightly grease a cookie sheet.

2 Sift the flour and salt into a mixing bowl. Stir in the sugar and yeast.

3 Rub the butter into the mixture using your fingers. Add all of the fruit juices and the water and mix to form a dough.

4 Place the dough on a lightly floured counter and knead for 5 minutes (alternatively, use an electric mixer with a dough hook). Place the dough in a greased bowl, cover, and let rise in a warm place for 1 hour.

5 Meanwhile, grate the rind of the orange, lemon, and lime. Knead the fruit rinds into the dough.

6 Divide the dough into 2 balls, one slightly bigger than the other.

7 Place the larger ball on the cookie sheet and place the smaller one on top.

8 Push a floured finger through the center of the dough. Cover and let rise for about 40 minutes or until springy to the touch.

9 Bake in a preheated oven at 425°F for 35 minutes. Remove from the oven and glaze with the honey.

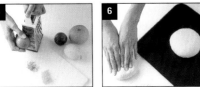

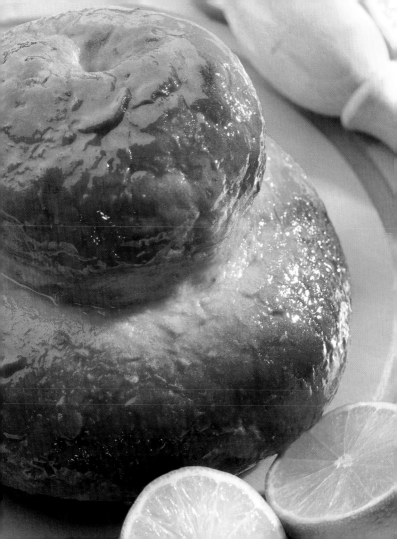

Mango Twist Bread

Makes 1 loaf

INGREDIENTS

4 cups strong white bread
    flour
1 tsp salt
1 packet active dry yeast
1 tsp ground ginger
3 tbsp light brown sugar
3 tbsp butter, cut into small
    pieces

1 small mango, peeled, cored,
    and puréed
generous 1 cup lukewarm
    water
2 tbsp clear honey
$2/3$ cup golden raisins

1 egg, beaten
confectioners' sugar,
    for dusting

1 Thoroughly grease a cookie sheet. Sift the flour and salt into a large mixing bowl and stir in the yeast, ground ginger, and brown sugar. Rub in the butter with your fingers.

2 Stir in the mango purée, water, and honey and mix together to form a dough.

3 Place the dough on a lightly floured surface and knead for about 5 minutes, until smooth (alternatively, use an electric mixer with a dough hook). Place the dough in a greased bowl, cover, and let rise in a warm place for about 1 hour, until it has doubled in size.

4 Knead in the golden raisins and shape the dough into 2 sausage shapes, each 10 inches long. Carefully twist the 2 pieces together and pinch the ends to seal. Place the dough on the cookie sheet, cover and let rise in a warm place for another 40 minutes.

5 Brush the loaf with the egg and bake in a preheated oven, at 425°F for 30 minutes, or until golden brown. Leave on a wire rack to cool completely. Dust with confectioners' sugar before serving.

Chocolate Bread

Makes 1 loaf

INGREDIENTS

4 cups strong white bread
   flour
$1/4$ cup unsweetened cocoa
1 tsp salt
1 packet active dry yeast

2 tbsp light brown sugar
1 tbsp oil
$1^1/2$ cups lukewarm water

1 Lightly grease a 2-pound loaf pan.

2 Sift the flour and the unsweetened cocoa into a large mixing bowl.

3 Stir in the salt, yeast, and brown sugar.

4 Pour in the oil along with the water and mix the ingredients together to make a dough.

5 Place the dough on a lightly floured surface and knead for about 5 minutes.

6 Place the dough in a greased bowl, cover, and let rise in a warm place for 1 hour, or until the dough has doubled in size.

7 Punch down the dough and shape it into a loaf. Place the dough into the prepared pan, cover, and then let rise in a warm place for a further 30 minutes.

8 Bake the dough in a preheated oven at 400°F for 25–30 minutes, or until a hollow sound can be heard when the base of the bread is tapped.

9 Transfer the chocolate bread to a wire rack and cool. Cut into slices to serve.

COOK'S TIP

This bread can be sliced and spread with butter or it can be lightly toasted.

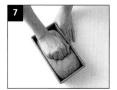

Soda Bread

Makes 1 loaf

INGREDIENTS

2¹/₂ cups whole-wheat flour
2¹/₂ cups all-purpose flour
2 tsp baking powder
1 tsp baking soda
2 tbsp superfine sugar

1 tsp salt
1 egg, beaten
1³/₄ cups unsweetened yogurt

1 Thoroughly grease and flour a cookie sheet.

2 Sift the flours, baking powder, baking soda, sugar, and salt into a large bowl.

3 In a mixing bowl, beat together the egg and yogurt and pour the mixture into the dry ingredients. Mix everything together to make a soft and sticky dough.

4 On a lightly floured surface, knead the dough for a few minutes until it is smooth, then shape into a round loaf about 2 inches deep.

5 Transfer the dough to the cookie sheet. Mark a cross shape in the center of the top of the dough.

6 Bake in a preheated oven at 375°F for about 40 minutes, or until the bread is golden brown.

7 Transfer the loaf to a wire rack and cool slightly before serving. Cut the soda bread into slices to serve.

VARIATION

For a delicious fruity version of this soda bread, add ³/₄ cup of raisins to the dry ingredients in step 2.

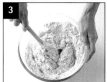

Spicy Bread

Makes 1 loaf

INGREDIENTS

2 cups self-rising flour	1 tsp baking powder	2 tsp poppy seeds
3/4 cup all-purpose flour	1/4 tsp salt	2 tbsp butter, cut into small
	1/4 tsp cayenne pepper	pieces
	2 tsp curry powder	2/3 cup milk
		1 egg, beaten

1 Grease a cookie sheet with butter.

2 Sift the self-rising flour and the all-purpose flour into a large mixing bowl, together with the baking powder, salt, cayenne pepper, curry powder, and poppy seeds.

3 Rub in the butter with your fingers until everything is well mixed together.

4 Add the milk and the beaten egg and mix to a soft dough.

5 Turn the dough out onto a lightly floured surface, then knead the dough lightly for a few minutes.

6 Shape the dough into a round loaf and mark it with a cross shape in the center of the top of the dough.

7 Bake in a preheated oven at 375°F for 45 minutes.

8 Transfer the bread to a wire rack and let cool. Serve in chunks or slices.

COOK'S TIP

If the bread looks as though it is browning too much, cover it with a piece of foil for the remainder of the cooking time.

Chili Corn Bread

Makes 12 bars

INGREDIENTS

1 cup all-purpose flour
1 cup cornmeal
1 tbsp baking powder
$^1/_2$ tsp salt

1 green chili, seeded and
finely chopped
5 scallions, finely chopped
2 eggs
generous $^1/_2$ cup sour cream

$^1/_2$ cup sunflower oil

1 Grease an 8-inch square cake pan and line the base with baking parchment.

2 In a large bowl, mix the flour, cornmeal, baking powder, and salt together.

3 Add the finely chopped green chili, and the scallions to the dry ingredients and mix until well combined.

4 In a large mixing bowl, beat the eggs, together with the sour cream and sunflower oil. Pour the mixture into the bowl of dry ingredients. Mix all of the ingredients together until well incorporated.

5 Pour the mixture into the prepared cake pan and level the surface with the back of a spoon.

6 Bake in a preheated oven at 400°F for 20–25 minutes, or until the loaf has risen and is lightly browned.

7 Let the bread cool slightly before turning out of the pan. Cut the bread into bars or squares to serve.

VARIATION

Add $^3/_4$ cup of corn kernels to the mixture in step 3, if you prefer.

Cheese & Potato Bread

Serves 4

INGREDIENTS

2 cups all-purpose flour	1/2 tsp mustard powder	2 cups cooked, mashed
1 tsp salt	2 tsp baking powder	potatoes
	1 cup grated Red Leicester	3/4 cup water
	cheese	1 tbsp oil

1 Lightly grease a cookie sheet.

2 Sift the flour, salt, mustard powder, and baking powder into a mixing bowl.

3 Reserve 2 tbsp of the grated cheese and stir the rest into the bowl with the mashed potatoes. Mix until well combined.

4 Pour in the water and the oil, and stir all the ingredients together (the mixture will be wet at this stage). Mix them all to make a soft dough.

5 Turn out the dough onto a floured surface and shape it into an 8-inch round loaf.

6 Place the loaf on the cookie sheet and mark it into 4 portions with a knife, without cutting through. Sprinkle with the reserved cheese.

7 Bake the loaf in a preheated oven at 425°F for approximately 25–30 minutes.

8 Transfer the bread to a wire rack and let cool. This bread should be served as fresh as possible.

COOK'S TIP

You can use instant potato mix for this bread, if you prefer.

VARIATION

Add 1/3 cup chopped ham to the mixture in step 3, if you prefer.

Cheese & Ham Loaf

Serves 6

INGREDIENTS

2 cups self-rising flour
1 tsp salt
2 tsp baking powder
1 tsp paprika
$^1/_3$ cup butter, cut into
small pieces

1 cup grated sharp cheese
$^1/_2$ cup smoked ham, chopped
2 eggs, beaten
$^2/_3$ cup milk

1 Thoroughly grease a 1-pound loaf pan and line the base with baking parchment.

2 Sift the flour, salt, baking powder, and paprika into a mixing bowl.

3 Rub in the butter with your fingers until the mixture resembles fine breadcrumbs. Stir in the cheese and ham.

4 Add the beaten eggs and milk to the dry ingredients and mix well.

5 Spoon the cheese and ham mixture into the prepared loaf pan.

6 Bake the mixture in a preheated oven at 350°F for about 1 hour, or until the loaf is well risen.

7 Let the bread cool in the pan, then turn out, and transfer to a wire rack to cool completely.

8 Serve the bread cut into thick slices.

COOK'S TIP

This tasty bread is best eaten on the day it is made, as it does not keep well for very long.

VARIATION

Any grated hard cheese can be used for this bread; use a milder one, if preferred.

Cheese & Chive Bread

Serves 8

INGREDIENTS

2 cups self-rising flour
1 tsp salt
1 tsp mustard powder
1 cup grated sharp cheese

2 tbsp chopped fresh chives
1 egg, beaten

2 tbsp butter, melted
²/3 cup milk

1 Grease a 9-inch square cake pan and line the base with baking parchment.

2 Sift the flour, salt, and mustard powder into a large mixing bowl.

3 Reserve 3 tbsp of the grated sharp cheese for sprinkling over the top of the loaf before baking in the oven.

4 Stir the remaining cheese into the bowl, together with the chopped fresh chives until well combined.

5 Add the beaten egg, melted butter, and milk and blend thoroughly.

6 Pour the mixture into the prepared pan and spread with a knife. Sprinkle with the reserved grated cheese.

7 Bake in a preheated oven at 375°F for about 30 minutes.

8 Let the bread cool slightly in the pan. Turn out the bread onto a wire rack to cool further before serving. Cut into triangles to serve.

COOK'S TIP

You can use any hard sharp cheese of your choice for this recipe.

Garlic Bread Rolls

Makes 8

INGREDIENTS

12 cloves garlic, peeled
1 1/2 cups milk
4 cups strong white
    bread flour
1 tsp salt

1 packet active dry yeast
1 tbsp dried mixed herbs
2 tbsp sunflower oil

1 egg, beaten
milk, for brushing
rock salt, for sprinkling

1 Grease a cookie sheet. Place the garlic cloves and milk in a saucepan, bring to a boil, and simmer gently for 15 minutes. Cool slightly, then process in a blender or food processor to purée the garlic.

2 Sift the flour and the 1 teaspoon of salt into a large mixing bowl and stir in the yeast and mixed herbs.

3 Add the garlic-flavored milk, sunflower oil, and beaten egg to the dry ingredients and mix everything to a dough.

4 Place the dough on a lightly floured counter and knead lightly for a few minutes until smooth and soft.

5 Place the dough in a greased bowl, cover, and let rise in a warm place for about 1 hour, or until doubled in size.

6 Punch down the dough by kneading it vigorously for 2 minutes. Shape into 8 rolls and place on the prepared cookie sheet. Lightly score the top of each roll with a knife, cover, and leave for 15 minutes.

7 Brush the rolls with a little milk and sprinkle rock salt over the top.

8 Bake in a preheated oven at 425°F for 15–20 minutes.

9 Transfer the rolls to a wire rack and cool completely before serving.

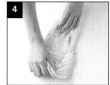

Mini Focaccia

Makes 4

INGREDIENTS

3 cups strong white flour
$^1/_2$ tsp salt
1 packet active dry yeast
2 tbsp olive oil

$1^1/_8$ cups lukewarm water
1 cup pitted green or black
   olives, halved

TOPPING:
2 red onions, sliced
2 tbsp olive oil
1 tsp sea salt
1 tbsp thyme leaves

1 Lightly oil several cookie sheets. Sift the flour and salt into a large mixing bowl, then stir in the yeast. Pour in the olive oil and water and mix everything together to form a dough.

2 Turn the dough out onto a lightly floured surface and knead it for 10 minutes.

3 Place the dough in a greased bowl, cover, and leave in a warm place for about 1–1$^1/_2$ hours, until it has doubled in size. Punch down the dough by kneading it again for 1–2 minutes.

4 Knead half of the olives into the dough. Divide the dough into quarters and then shape the quarters into rounds. Place them on the cookie sheets and push your fingers into the dough to achieve a dimpled effect.

5 To make the topping, sprinkle the red onions and remaining olives over the rounds. Drizzle the olive oil over the top and sprinkle with the sea salt and thyme. Cover and let the dough rise again for 30 minutes.

6 Bake in a preheated oven at 375°F for 20–25 minutes, or until the focaccia are well cooked and golden. Transfer to a wire rack and cool before serving.

Sun-dried Tomato Rolls

Makes 8

INGREDIENTS

2 cups strong white
   bread flour
$^1/_2$ tsp salt
1 packet active dry yeast

$^1/_3$ cup butter, melted and
   cooled slightly
3 tbsp milk, warmed
2 eggs, beaten

1 cup drained and finely
   chopped sun-dried
   tomatoes
milk, for brushing

1 Lightly grease a cookie sheet.

2 Sift the flour and salt into a large mixing bowl. Stir in the yeast, then pour in the butter, milk, and eggs. Mix together to form a dough.

3 Turn the dough onto a lightly floured surface and knead for about 5 minutes (alternatively, use an electric mixer with a dough hook).

4 Place the dough in a greased bowl, cover, and let rise in a warm place for 1–1$^1/_2$ hours, until the dough has doubled in size. Punch down the dough by kneading it lightly for a few minutes.

5 Knead the sun-dried tomatoes into the dough, sprinkling the counter with extra flour as the tomatoes are quite oily.

6 Divide the dough into 8 balls and place them on the prepared cookie sheet. Cover and let rise for about 30 minutes, until the rolls have doubled in size.

7 Lightly brush the rolls with a little milk and bake in a preheated oven, at 450°F for 10–15 minutes, until the rolls are golden brown.

8 Transfer the rolls to a wire rack and cool slightly before serving.

Thyme Crescents

Makes 8

INGREDIENTS

9 ounces fresh ready-made
    puff pastry
$1/3$ cup butter, softened
1 garlic clove, crushed

1 tsp lemon juice
1 tsp dried thyme
salt and pepper

1 Lightly grease a cookie sheet.

2 On a lightly floured surface, roll out the pastry dough to form a 10-inch round and cut into 8 wedges.

3 In a small bowl, mix together the softened butter, garlic clove, lemon juice, and dried thyme until soft. Season to taste.

4 Spread a little of the butter and thyme mixture onto each wedge of pastry dough, dividing it equally between them.

5 Carefully roll up each wedge of pastry dough, starting from the wide end.

6 Arrange the crescents on the prepared cookie sheet and chill for about 30 minutes.

7 Dampen the cookie sheet with cold water. This will create a steamy atmosphere in the oven while the crescents are baking and help the pastries to rise.

8 Bake in a preheated oven at 400°F for 10–15 minutes, until the crescents are well risen and golden.

COOK'S TIP

Dried herbs have a stronger flavor than fresh ones, which makes them perfect for these pastries. The crescents can be made with other dried herbs of your choice, such as rosemary and sage, or mixed herbs.

Cheese & Mustard Scones

Makes 8

INGREDIENTS

2 cups self-rising flour
1 tsp baking powder
pinch of salt
1/3 cup butter, cut into small
  pieces

1 cup grated sharp cheese
1 tsp mustard powder

2/3 cup milk
pepper

1 Lightly grease a cookie sheet.

2 Sift the flour, baking powder, and salt into a mixing bowl. Rub in the butter with your fingers until the mixture resembles breadcrumbs.

3 Stir in the grated cheese, mustard, and enough milk to form a soft dough.

4 On a lightly floured surface, knead the dough very lightly, then flatten it out with the palm of your hand to a depth of about 1 inch.

5 Cut the dough into 8 wedges with a knife. Brush each one with a little milk and sprinkle with pepper to taste.

6 Bake in a preheated oven at 425°F for 10–15 minutes, until the scones are a golden brown.

7 Transfer the scones to a wire rack and cool slightly before serving.

COOK'S TIP

Scones should be eaten on the day they are made, as they quickly go stale. Serve them split in half and spread with butter.

Cheese Sables

Makes about 35

INGREDIENTS

1¼ cups all-purpose flour
1½ cup grated sharp cheese

⅔ cup butter, cut into
small pieces
1 egg yolk
sesame seeds, for sprinkling

1 Lightly grease several cookie sheets.

2 Mix the flour and cheese together in a bowl.

3 Add the butter to the cheese and flour mixture and mix with your fingers until combined.

4 Stir in the egg yolk and mix to form a dough. Wrap the dough and chill in the refrigerator for about 30 minutes.

5 On a lightly floured surface, roll out the cheese dough thinly. Cut out 2½-inch rounds, re-rolling the trimmings to make about 35 rounds.

6 Place the rounds onto the prepared cookie sheets and sprinkle the sesame seeds over the top of them.

7 Bake in a preheated oven at 400°F for 20 minutes, until the sables are a light golden color.

8 Transfer the cheese sables to a wire rack and cool slightly before serving.

COOK'S TIP

Cut out any shape you like for your savory biscuits. Children will enjoy them cut into animal or other fun shapes.

Savory Curried Biscuits

Makes 40

INGREDIENTS

³/4 cup all-purpose flour
1 tsp salt
2 tsp curry powder
1 cup grated mellow hard
  cheese

1 cup grated Parmesan cheese
¹/3 cup butter, softened

1 Lightly grease about 4 cookie sheets with butter.

2 Sift the all-purpose flour and salt into a mixing bowl.

3 Add the curry powder, the grated mellow hard cheese, and the grated Parmesan cheese to the mixing bowl and stir until well incorporated. Rub in the softened butter with your fingertips until the mixture comes together to form a soft dough.

4 On a lightly floured surface, roll out the dough thinly to form a rectangle.

5 Using a 2-inch cutter, cut out 40 round biscuits.

6 Arrange the biscuits on the cookie sheets.

7 Bake in a preheated oven at 350°F for 10–15 minutes.

8 Let the biscuits cool slightly on the cookie sheets.

9 Transfer the biscuits to a wire rack until cold and crisp, then serve.

COOK'S TIP

These biscuits can be stored for several days in an airtight metal or plastic container.

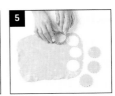

Cheese Pudding

Serves 4

INGREDIENTS

2¹/₂ cups fresh white
   breadcrumbs
1 cup grated Swiss cheese
²/₃ cup lukewarm milk
¹/₂ cup butter, melted

2 eggs, separated
2 tbsp chopped fresh parsley
salt and pepper
salad greens, to serve

1 Thoroughly grease a 5 cup ovenproof dish.

2 Place the breadcrumbs and cheese in a bowl and mix.

3 Pour the milk over the cheese and breadcrumb mixture and stir to mix. Add the melted butter, egg yolks, parsley, and salt and pepper to taste. Mix well.

4 Whisk the egg whites until firm. Fold the cheese mixture into the egg whites.

5 Transfer the mixture to the prepared ovenproof dish.

6 Bake the pudding in a preheated oven at 375°F for about 45 minutes or until golden brown, and slightly risen, and a knife inserted into the middle of the pudding comes out clean.

7 Serve the cheese pudding hot, with salad greens.

VARIATION

Any strongly flavored cheese of your choice can be used instead of the Swiss cheese to make this tasty savory pudding.

COOK'S TIP

For a slightly healthier alternative, make the cheese pudding with fresh whole-wheat breadcrumbs instead of white ones.

Cheese & Onion Pies

Makes 4

INGREDIENTS

3 tbsp vegetable oil
4 onions, peeled and finely
    sliced
4 garlic cloves, crushed
4 tbsp finely chopped fresh
    parsley
3/4 cup grated sharp cheese

salt and pepper

PIE DOUGH:
1 1/2 cups all-purpose flour
1/2 tsp salt
1/3 cup butter, cut into
    small pieces
3–4 tbsp water

1 Heat the oil in a skillet. Add the onions and garlic and sauté for 10–15 minutes, or until the onions are soft. Remove the pan from the heat and stir in the parsley and cheese, and season.

2 To make the pie dough, sift the flour and salt into a mixing bowl and rub in the butter with your fingertips until the mixture resembles breadcrumbs. Stir in the water and mix to a smooth dough.

3 On a lightly floured surface, roll out the dough and divide it into 8 portions.

4 Roll out each portion to a 4-inch round and use half of the rounds to line 4 individual tart pans.

5 Fill each round with a quarter of the onion mixture. Cover with the remaining 4 pie dough rounds. Make a slit in the top of each pie with the point of a knife and seal the edges with the back of a teaspoon.

6 Bake in a preheated oven at 425°F for about 20 minutes. The pies can be served hot or cold.

COOK'S TIP

You can prepare the onion filling in advance and store it in the refrigerator.

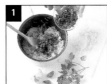

Red Onion Tart Tatin

Serves 4

INGREDIENTS

4 tbsp butter

2 tbsp sugar

1 pound 2 ounces red onions,
    peeled and quartered

3 tbsp red wine vinegar

2 tbsp fresh thyme leaves

8 ounces fresh ready-made
    puff pastry

salt and pepper

1 Place the butter and sugar in a 9-inch ovenproof skillet and cook over a medium heat until the butter has melted.

2 Add the red onion quarters and sweat them over a low heat for 10–15 minutes, until golden, stirring occasionally.

3 Add the red wine vinegar and fresh thyme leaves to the skillet. Season with salt and pepper to taste, then simmer over a medium heat until the liquid has reduced and the red onion pieces are coated in the buttery sauce.

4 On a lightly floured kitchen counter, roll out the pastry to a round slightly larger than the skillet.

5 Place the dough over the onion mixture and press down, tucking in the edges to seal the pie dough.

6 Bake in a preheated oven at 350°F for about 20–25 minutes. Let the tart stand for 10 minutes.

7 To turn out, place a serving plate over the skillet and carefully invert them both so that the dough crust becomes the base of the tart. Serve the tart warm.

VARIATION

Replace the red onions with shallots, leaving them whole, if you prefer.

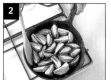

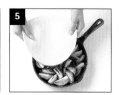

Puff Potato Pie

Serves 6

INGREDIENTS

1 pound 9 ounces potatoes,
    peeled and thinly sliced
2 scallions, finely chopped
1 red onion, finely chopped
$^2/_3$ cup heavy cream

1 pound 2 ounces fresh ready-
    made puff pastry
2 eggs, beaten
salt and pepper

1 Lightly grease a cookie sheet. Bring a pan of water to a boil, add the sliced potatoes, bring back to a boil, and then simmer for a few minutes. Drain the potato and cool. Dry off any excess moisture with paper towels.

2 In a bowl, mix together the scallions, red onion, and the cooled potato slices. Stir in 2 tablespoons of the cream and plenty of seasoning.

3 Divide the pastry in half and roll out one piece to a 9-inch round. Roll the remaining dough to a 10-inch round.

4 Place the smaller round onto the cookie sheet and top with the potato mixture, leaving a 1-inch border all around. Brush this border with a little of the beaten egg.

5 Top with the larger round of dough, seal well, and crimp the edges of the dough. Cut a steam vent in the middle of the dough and, using the back of a knife, mark with a pattern. Brush with the beaten egg and bake in a preheated oven at 400°F for 30 minutes.

6 Mix the remaining beaten egg with the rest of the cream and pour into the pie through the steam vent. Return the pie to the oven for 15 minutes. Serve either warm or cold.

Fresh Tomato Tarts

Serves 6

INGREDIENTS

9 ounces fresh ready-made
    puff pastry
1 egg, beaten
2 tbsp pesto

6 plum tomatoes, sliced
salt and pepper

fresh thyme leaves, to garnish
(optional)

1 On a lightly floured kitchen counter, roll out the pastry dough to a rectangle measuring 12 × 10 inches.

2 Cut the rectangle in half and divide each half into 3 pieces to make 6 even-size rectangles. Chill in the refrigerator for 20 minutes.

3 Lightly score the edges of the dough rectangles and brush with the beaten egg.

4 Spread the pesto over the rectangles, dividing it equally between them, leaving a 1-inch border on each one.

5 Arrange the tomato slices in a line along the center of each rectangle on top of the pesto.

6 Season well with salt and pepper to taste and lightly sprinkle with fresh thyme leaves, if using.

7 Bake in a preheated oven at 400°F for 15–20 minutes, until well risen and a golden brown color.

8 Transfer the tomato tarts to warm serving plates straight from the oven and serve while they are still piping hot.

VARIATION

Instead of making individual tarts, roll the dough out to form 1 large rectangle. Spoon the pesto on and arrange the tomatoes over the top.

Provençal Tart

Serves 6–8

INGREDIENTS

9 ounces ready-made fresh
   puff pastry
3 tbsp olive oil
2 red bell peppers, seeded and
   diced

2 green bell peppers, seeded
   and diced
2/3 cup heavy cream

1 egg
2 zucchini, sliced
salt and pepper

1 Roll out the pastry on a lightly floured surface and line an 8-inch loose-bottomed quiche pan. Chill in the refrigerator for 20 minutes.

2 Meanwhile, heat 2 tbsp of the olive oil in a skillet and sauté the bell peppers for about 8 minutes, until softened, stirring frequently.

3 Whisk the heavy cream and egg together in a large mixing bowl and season to taste with salt and pepper. Stir in the cooked mixed bell peppers.

4 Heat the remaining oil in a pan and fry the zucchini slices for 4–5 minutes, until they are lightly browned.

5 Carefully pour the egg and bell pepper mixture into the pie shell.

6 Arrange the zucchini slices in a pattern around the edge of the tart.

7 Bake in a preheated oven at 350°F for 35–40 minutes, or until just set and golden brown. Serve hot or cold.

COOK'S TIP

This recipe could be used to make 6 individual tarts—use 6 × 4 inch pans and bake them for 20 minutes.

Celery & Onion Pies

Makes 12

INGREDIENTS

PIE DOUGH:
1 cup all-purpose flour
1/2 tsp salt
2 tbsp butter, cut into
    small pieces

1/4 cup grated sharp cheese
3–4 tbsp water

FILLING:
4 tbsp butter
1 cup finely chopped celery
2 garlic cloves, crushed
1 small onion, finely chopped

1 tbsp all-purpose flour
1/4 cup milk
salt
pinch of cayenne pepper

1 To make the filling, melt the butter, add the celery, garlic, and onion and sauté for 5 minutes, or until softened.

2 Remove from the heat and stir in the flour, then the milk. Heat gently until the mixture is thick, stirring frequently. Season with salt and cayenne pepper. Let cool.

3 To make the pastry, sift together the flour and salt into a mixing bowl and rub in the butter with your fingertips. Stir the cheese into the mixture, together with the cold water, and mix to form a dough.

4 Roll out three-quarters of the dough. Using a 2½-inch cookie cutter, cut out 12 rounds. Line a muffin pan with the rounds.

5 Divide the filling between the pie dough rounds. Roll out the remaining dough and, using a 2-inch cutter, cut out 12 rounds. Place the smaller rounds on top of the pie filling and seal well. Make a slit in each pie and chill for 30 minutes.

6 Bake in a preheated oven at 425°F for 15–20 minutes. Cool in the pan for about 10 minutes before turning out. Serve warm.

Asparagus & Goat Cheese Tart

Serves 6

INGREDIENTS

9 ounces fresh ready-made pie dough	1/4 cup chopped hazelnuts	4 tbsp light cream
9 ounces asparagus	1 3/4 cups ounces goat cheese	salt and pepper
1 tbsp vegetable oil	2 eggs, beaten	
1 red onion, finely chopped		

1 On a lightly floured surface, roll out the pie dough and line a 10-inch loose-bottomed quiche pan. Prick the base of the pie dough with a fork and chill in the refrigerator for about 30 minutes.

2 Line the pie shell with foil and dried beans and bake blind in a preheated oven at 375°F for approximately 15 minutes.

3 Remove the foil and beans from the pie shell, return the pie shell to the oven and cook it for a further 15 minutes.

4 Cook the asparagus in boiling water for 2–3 minutes, drain, and cut into bite-size pieces.

5 Heat the oil in a small skillet and sauté the onion until soft. Spoon the asparagus, onion, and chopped hazelnuts into the prepared pie shell.

6 Beat together the cheese, eggs, and cream until smooth, or process in a blender until smooth.

Season well with salt and pepper, then pour the mixture over the asparagus, onion, and hazelnuts.

7 Bake in the oven for 15–20 minutes, or until the cheese filling is just set. Serve warm or cold.

VARIATION

Omit the hazelnuts and sprinkle Parmesan cheese over the top of the tart just before cooking in the oven, if you prefer.

Onion Tart

Serves 6

INGREDIENTS

9 ounces fresh ready-made
    shortcrust pie dough
3 tbsp butter
1/2 cup diced bacon

1 pound 9 ounces onions,
    peeled and sliced thinly
2 eggs, beaten
2/3 cup grated Parmesan
    cheese

1 tsp dried sage
salt and pepper

1 Roll out the pie dough on a lightly floured counter and line a 10-inch loose-bottomed quiche pan.

2 Prick the base of the pie dough all over with a fork and chill for 30 minutes.

3 Heat the butter in a saucepan, add the diced bacon and sliced onions, and sweat them over a low heat for about 25 minutes, or until tender. If the onion slices start to turn brown, add a tablespoon of water to the saucepan.

4 Add the beaten eggs to the onion mixture and stir in the cheese, sage, and salt and pepper to taste. Mix until well combined.

5 Carefully spoon the onion mixture into the prepared pie shell, spreading the mixture to the edges of the shell.

6 Bake in a preheated oven at 350°F for 20–30 minutes, or until the tart has just set.

7 Leave the tart to cool slightly in the pan, then serve the onion tart warm or cold. Cut the tart into slices to serve.

VARIATION

For a vegetarian version, replace the bacon with the same quantity of chopped mushrooms.

Pissaladière

Serves 8

INGREDIENTS

4 tbsp olive oil
1 pound 9 ounces red onions, thinly sliced
2 garlic cloves, crushed
2 tsp superfine sugar

2 tbsp red wine vinegar
12 ounces fresh ready-made puff pastry
salt and pepper

TOPPING:
2 1¾-ounce cans anchovy fillets
12 pitted green olives
1 tsp dried marjoram

1 Lightly grease a jelly roll pan with butter. Heat the olive oil in a large saucepan. Add the onions and garlic and cook over a very low heat for about 30 minutes, stirring occasionally, until tender.

2 Add the sugar and vinegar to the pan and season with plenty of salt and pepper to taste. Stir until well combined.

3 On a lightly floured surface, roll out the pastry dough to a rectangle about 13 × 9 inches. Place the dough rectangle onto the prepared jelly roll pan, pushing the dough well into the corners of the pan.

4 Spread the onion mixture over the dough.

5 Top with the anchovy fillets and green olives, then sprinkle with the marjoram.

6 Bake in a preheated oven at 425°F for about 20–25 minutes, until the pissaladière is a light golden color. Serve piping hot, straight from the oven.

VARIATION

Cut the pissaladière into squares or triangles for easy finger food at a party or barbecue.

Mini Cheese & Onion Tarts

Serves 12

INGREDIENTS

PIE DOUGH:
1 cup all-purpose flour
$1/4$ tsp salt
$1/3$ cup butter, cut into small pieces
1–2 tbsp water

FILLING:
1 egg, beaten
generous $1/3$ cup light cream
$1/2$ cup grated Red Leicester cheese,
3 scallions, finely chopped
salt

cayenne pepper

1 To make the pie dough, sift the flour and salt into a mixing bowl. Rub in the butter with your fingers until well combined and the mixture resembles fine breadcrumbs. Gradually stir in the water, adding little by little, and mix to form a smooth dough.

2 Roll out the pie dough on a lightly floured kitchen surface. Using a 3-inch cookie cutter, stamp out 12 rounds from the dough and line a muffin pan.

3 To make the filling, whisk together the beaten egg, light cream, grated Red Leicester cheese, and chopped scallions. Season with salt and cayenne.

4 Pour the filling mixture into the pie shells and bake in a preheated oven at 350°F for about 20–25 minutes, or until the filling is just set.

5 Serve the mini tarts warm or cold.

VARIATION

Top each mini tart with slices of fresh tomato before baking, if you prefer.

COOK'S TIP

If you use 6 ounces of ready-made pie dough instead of making it yourself, these tarts can be made in minutes.

Ham & Cheese Lattice Pies

Makes 6

INGREDIENTS

9 ounces fresh ready-made
    puff pastry
1/3 cup finely chopped ham
2/3 cup full-fat soft cheese

2 tbsp chopped fresh chives
1 egg, beaten

2 tbsp freshly grated
    Parmesan cheese
pepper

1 Roll out the pastry thinly on a lightly floured counter. Cut out 12 rectangles measuring 6 × 2 inches.

2 Place the rectangles onto greased cookie sheets and leave to chill for 30 minutes.

3 Meanwhile, combine the ham, cheese, and chives in a small bowl. Season with pepper to taste.

4 Spread the ham and cheese mixture along the center of 6 of the rectangles, leaving a 1-inch border around each one. Brush the border with a little beaten egg.

5 To make the lattice pattern, fold the remaining rectangles lengthwise. Leaving a 1-inch border, cut vertical lines across one edge of the rectangles using a sharp knife.

6 Unfold the rectangles and place them over the rectangles topped with the ham and cheese mixture set on the cookie sheets. Seal the dough edges well and lightly sprinkle with the grated Parmesan cheese.

7 Bake in a preheated oven at 350°F for 15–20 minutes. Serve hot or cold.

COOK'S TIP

These pies can be made in advance, frozen uncooked, and baked fresh when required.

Vegetarian Baking

The variety of recipes in this chapter will allow vegetarians and vegans to enjoy baking recipes and to experiment with the fillings and toppings to suit their individuals needs. Some of the recipes include variations of family classics, such as Pineapple Upside-down Cake, Fruit Crumble, and Date & Apricot Tart.

Most supermarkets and health food stores stock a variety of products to cater for vegetarians' dietary needs and preferences. Useful products include soy milk, which is sold in concentrated form that needs diluting, ready-to-drink form, or in powdered form; and cooking fats, including various brands of vegan margarine and numerous white vegetable fats which are ideal for pastries and frying.

Bean curd is a versatile, whitish, curd-like product, high in protein and cholesterol-free, which can be used in sweet and savory dishes.

This chapter includes recipes for eggless sponges which are made by adding extra liquid (usually oil) and increasing the amount of rising agent.

Curry Turnovers

Serves 4

INGREDIENTS

$1^3/_4$ cups plain whole-wheat flour	$1^1/_4$ cups diced root vegetables (potatoes, carrots, and parsnips)	$1/_2$ tsp ground cumin
$1/_3$ cup vegan margarine, cut into small pieces	1 small onion, chopped	$1/_2$ tsp wholegrain mustard
4 tbsp water	2 garlic cloves, finely chopped	5 tbsp stock
2 tbsp oil	$1/_2$ tsp curry powder	soy milk, to glaze
	$1/_2$ tsp ground turmeric	

1 Place the flour in a mixing bowl and rub in the vegan margarine with your fingertips until the mixture resembles breadcrumbs. Stir in the water and bring together to form a soft dough. Wrap and chill in the refrigerator for 30 minutes.

2 To make the filling, heat the oil in a large saucepan. Add the diced root vegetables, chopped onion, and garlic. Sauté for 2 minutes, then stir in all of the spices, turning the vegetables to coat them with the spices. Cook for a further 1 minute.

3 Add the stock to the pan and bring to a boil. Cover and simmer for about 20 minutes, stirring occasionally, until the vegetables are tender and the liquid has been absorbed. Let cool.

4 Divide the pie dough into 4 portions. Roll each portion into a 6-inch round. Place the filling equally on one half of each round.

5 Brush the edges of each round with soy milk, then fold over and press the edges together to seal. Place on a cookie sheet. Bake in a preheated oven at 400°F for 25-30 minutes, until the pastry is a light golden brown color.

Brazil Nut & Mushroom Pie

Serves 4–6

INGREDIENTS

PIE DOUGH:
$1^3/4$ cups plain whole-wheat
    flour
$1/3$ cup vegan margarine, cut
    into small pieces
4 tbsp water
soy milk, to glaze

FILLING:
2 tbsp vegan margarine
1 onion, chopped
1 garlic clove, finely chopped
2 cups sliced button
    mushrooms
1 tbsp all-purpose flour
$2/3$ cup vegetable stock
1 tbsp tomato paste
$1^1/2$ cups chopped Brazil nuts

$1^1/3$ cups fresh whole-wheat
    breadcrumbs
2 tbsp chopped fresh parsley
$1/2$ tsp pepper

1 To make the pie dough, rub the margarine into the flour until it resembles fine breadcrumbs. Stir in the water and bring together to form a dough. Wrap and chill for 30 minutes.

2 Melt the margarine for the filling in a skillet, add the onion, garlic, and mushrooms and sauté for 5 minutes, until softened. Add the flour and cook for 1 minute, stirring. Gradually add the stock, stirring until the sauce is smooth and beginning to thicken. Stir in the tomato paste, Brazil nuts, breadcrumbs, parsley, and pepper. Cool slightly.

3 On a lightly floured surface, roll out two-thirds of the pie dough and use to line an 8-inch loose-bottomed quiche pan or pie dish. Spread the filling in the pie shell. Brush the edges of the pie dough with soy milk. Roll out the remaining pie dough to fit the top of the pie. Seal the edges, make a slit in the top of the pie dough, and brush with soy milk.

4 Bake in a preheated oven at 400°F for 30–40 minutes, until golden brown.

Lentil & Red Bell Pepper Flan

Serves 6–8

INGREDIENTS

PIE DOUGH:
1³/₄ cups plain whole-wheat
    flour
¹/₃ cup vegan margarine, cut
    into small pieces
4 tbsp water

FILLING:
³/₄ cup red lentils, rinsed
1¹/₄ cups vegetable stock
1 tbsp vegan margarine
1 onion, chopped
2 red bell peppers, cored,
    seeded, and diced
1 tsp yeast extract

1 tbsp tomato paste
3 tbsp chopped fresh parsley
pepper

1 To make the pie dough, place the flour in a mixing bowl and rub in the vegan margarine with your fingertips until the mixture resembles fine breadcrumbs. Stir in the water and bring together to form a dough. Wrap and chill in the refrigerator for 30 minutes.

2 Meanwhile, make the filling. Put the lentils in a saucepan with the stock, bring to a boil, and then simmer for 10 minutes, until the lentils are tender and can be mashed to a purée.

3 Melt the margarine in a small pan, add the chopped onion and diced red bell peppers and sauté until just soft.

4 Add the lentil purée, yeast extract, tomato paste, and parsley. Season with pepper. Mix until well combined.

5 On a lightly floured kitchen counter, roll out the dough and line a 10-inch loose-bottomed quiche pan. Prick the base of the pie dough with a fork and spoon the lentil purée mixture into the pie shell.

6 Bake in a preheated oven at 400°F for 30 minutes, until the filling is firm.

Garlic & Sage Bread

Serves 4–6

INGREDIENTS

2¼ cups strong brown bread flour	2 tsp sea salt	1 tsp honey
1 sachet active dry yeast	3 garlic cloves, finely chopped	⅔ cup lukewarm water
3 tbsp chopped fresh sage		

1 Grease a cookie sheet. Sift the flour into a large mixing bowl and stir in the husks remaining in the strainer.

2 Stir in the yeast, sage, and half of the sea salt. Reserve 1 teaspoon of the chopped garlic for sprinkling and stir the rest into the bowl. Add the honey with the water and mix together to form a dough.

3 Turn the dough out onto a lightly floured surface and knead it for about 5 minutes

(alternatively, use an electric mixer with a dough hook).

4 Place the dough in a greased bowl, cover, and let rise in a warm place until it has doubled in size.

5 Knead the dough again for a few minutes, shape it into a round (see Cook's Tip) and place on the cookie sheet.

6 Cover and let rise for a further 30 minutes, or until springy to the touch. Sprinkle with the rest of the sea salt and garlic.

7 Bake in a preheated oven at 400°F for 25–30 minutes. Cool on a wire rack before serving.

Apricot Slices

Makes 12

INGREDIENTS

PIE DOUGH:
1³/4 cups whole-wheat flour
¹/2 cup finely ground mixed
    nuts
¹/3 cup vegan margarine, cut
    into small pieces
4 tbsp water

soy milk, to glaze

FILLING:
2 cups dried apricots
grated rind of 1 orange
1¹/3 cups apple juice
1 tsp ground cinnamon
¹/3 cup raisins

1 Lightly grease a 9-inch square cake pan. To make the pie dough, place the flour and nuts in a mixing bowl and rub in the margarine with your fingers until the mixture resembles breadcrumbs. Stir in the water and bring together to form a dough. Wrap and chill for 30 minutes.

2 To make the filling, place the apricots, orange rind, and apple juice in a saucepan and bring to a boil. Simmer for 30 minutes, until the apricots are mushy. Cool slightly, then blend to a purée. Stir in the ground cinnamon and raisins.

3 Divide the pie dough in half, roll out one half, and use to line the base of the pan. Spread the apricot purée over the top and brush the edges of the pie dough with water. Roll out the rest of the dough to fit over the top of the apricot purée. Press down, sealing the edges with a teaspoon.

4 Prick the top of the pie dough with a fork and brush with a little soy milk. Bake in a preheated oven at 400°F for 20–25 minutes, until the pastry is a golden color. Cool slightly before cutting into 12 bars. Serve warm or cold.

Baked Bean Curd Cheesecake

Serves 6

INGREDIENTS

2¹/2 cups crushed graham
    crackers
4 tbsp vegan margarine,
    melted
¹/4 cups pitted, chopped dates
4 tbsp lemon juice
rind of 1 lemon

3 tbsp water
12 ounces firm bean curd
²/3 cup apple juice
1 banana, mashed
1 tsp vanilla extract
1 mango, peeled and chopped

1 Lightly grease a 7-inch round loose-bottomed cake pan with a little butter.

2 Mix together the graham cracker crumbs and melted margarine in a bowl. Press the mixture into the base of the prepared pan.

3 Put the chopped dates, lemon juice, lemon rind, and water into a saucepan and bring to a boil. Simmer for 5 minutes until the dates are soft, then mash them roughly with a fork.

4 Place the mixture in a blender or food processor with the bean curd, apple juice, mashed banana, and vanilla extract and process until the mixture is a thick, smooth purée.

5 Pour the bean curd purée into the prepared graham cracker crumb base.

6 Bake in a preheated oven at 350°F for 30–40 minutes, until lightly golden in color. Cool in the pan, then chill thoroughly before serving.

7 Place the chopped mango in a blender and process until smooth. Serve it as a sauce with the chilled cheesecake.

Pineapple Upside-down Cake

Serves 6

INGREDIENTS

15 ounce can unsweetened
    pineapple pieces, drained
    and juice reserved
4 tsp cornstarch
3 tbsp light brown sugar
4 tbsp vegan margarine, cut
    into small pieces
$^1/_2$ cup water
rind of 1 lemon

SPONGE:
$^1/_4$ cup sunflower oil
$^1/_3$ cup light brown sugar
$^2/_3$ cup water
$1^1/_4$ cups all-purpose flour
2 tsp baking powder
1 tsp ground cinnamon

1 Grease a deep 7-inch cake pan. Mix the reserved juice from the pineapple with the cornstarch until it forms a smooth paste. Put the paste in a saucepan with the sugar, vegan margarine, and water and stir over a low heat until the sugar has dissolved. Bring to a boil and simmer for 2–3 minutes, until thickened. Cool the mixture slightly.

2 To make the sponge, place the oil, sugar, and water in a saucepan. Heat gently until the sugar has dissolved; do not allow it to boil. Remove from the heat and cool. Sift the flour, baking powder, and ground cinnamon into a mixing bowl. Add the cooled sugar syrup and beat well to form a batter.

3 Place the pineapple pieces and lemon rind on the bottom of the pan and pour 4 tbsp of the pineapple syrup over the pineapple. Spoon the sponge batter on top.

4 Bake in a preheated oven at 350°F for 35–40 minutes, until set and a knife inserted into the center comes out clean. Invert onto a plate, let stand for 5 minutes, then remove the pan. Serve the cake with the remaining syrup.

Date & Apricot Tart

Serves 6–8

INGREDIENTS

1¾ cups plain whole-wheat flour
½ cup ground mixed nuts
⅓ cup vegan margarine, cut into small pieces

4 tbsp water
2 cups dried apricots, chopped
1⅓ cups pitted, chopped dates
2 cups apple juice
1 tsp ground cinnamon
grated rind of 1 lemon
soy custard, to serve (optional)

1 Place the flour and ground nuts in a mixing bowl and rub in the margarine with your fingertips until the mixture resembles breadcrumbs. Stir in the water and bring together to form a dough. Wrap the dough and chill for 30 minutes.

2 Meanwhile, place the apricots and dates in a saucepan with the apple juice, cinnamon, and lemon rind. Bring to a boil, cover, and simmer for 15 minutes, until the fruit softens and can be mashed to a purée.

3 Reserve a small ball of pie dough for making lattice strips. On a lightly floured surface, roll out the rest of the dough to form a round and use to line a 9-inch loose-bottomed quiche pan.

4 Spread the fruit filling over the base of the pie dough. Roll out the reserved pie dough and cut into strips ½ inch wide. Cut the strips to fit the tart and twist them across the top of the fruit to form a lattice pattern. Moisten the edges of the strips with water and seal to the rim.

5 Bake in a preheated oven at 400°F for 25–30 minutes, until golden brown. Cut into slices and serve with soy custard, if using.

2

4

4

Fruit Crumble

Serves 6

INGREDIENTS

6 eating pears, peeled, cored,
    quartered, and sliced
1 tbsp chopped preserved
    ginger
1 tbsp molasses
2 tbsp orange juice

TOPPING:
1 1/2 cups all-purpose flour
1/3 cup vegan margarine, cut
    into small pieces
1/4 cup slivered almonds
1/3 cup dried oats
1/8 cup molasses

soy custard, to serve

1 Lightly grease a 5 cup ovenproof dish.

2 In a bowl, mix together the pears, ginger, molasses, and orange juice. Spoon the mixture into the prepared dish.

3 To make the crumble topping, sift the flour into a mixing bowl and rub in the margarine with your fingers until well combined and the mixture resembles fine breadcrumbs. Stir in the slivered almonds, oats, and molasses. Mix together until all the ingredients are well combined.

4 Sprinkle the crumble topping evenly over the pear and ginger mixture in the dish, to cover the fruit completely.

5 Bake the crumble in a preheated oven at 375°F for 30 minutes, until the topping is golden and the fruit is tender.

Serve with soy custard, if using.

VARIATION

*Stir 1 tsp apple
pie spice into the
crumble mixture in
step 3 for added flavor,
if you prefer.*

Eggless Sponge Cake

Makes one 8-inch cake

INGREDIENTS

1 3/4 cups self-rising whole-
    wheat flour
2 tsp baking powder
3/4 cup superfine sugar
6 tbsp sunflower oil

1 cup water
1 tsp vanilla extract
4 tbsp strawberry or raspberry
    reduced-sugar spread

superfine sugar, for dusting

1 Thoroughly grease two 8-inch layer pans with butter and line them with baking parchment.

2 Sift the flour and baking powder into a large mixing bowl, stirring in any bran remaining in the strainer. Stir in the superfine sugar.

3 Pour in the oil, water, and vanilla extract and mix together with a wooden spoon for about 1 minute until the cake mixture is a smooth consistency.

4 Divide the mixture between the prepared pans, levelling the surface with the back of a spoon.

5 Bake in a preheated oven at 350°F for 25–30 minutes, until the center springs back when lightly touched. Leave to cool in the pans before turning out and transferring to a wire rack.

6 To serve the cake, remove the baking parchment and place one of the sponges onto a serving plate. Cover with the strawberry or raspberry spread and place the other sponge on top. Dust with a little superfine sugar and cut into slices.

VARIATION

Use melted vegan butter or margarine instead of the sunflower oil if you prefer, but allow it to cool before adding it to the dry ingredients in step 3.

Cakes

This chapter includes a variety of different cakes, depending on the time you have and the effort you want to spend. Small cakes include Gingerbread, Carrot Squares, and White Chocolate & Apricot Squares. These cakes are easier to prepare and cook than larger ones and, in general, are particular favorites to have with a cup of coffee or to provide for a child's school lunch.

Cakes such as Almond Cake and Lemon Syrup Cake are made very quickly using baking powder, which produces quick, well-risen cakes.

Others require special ingredients to produce cakes with that "little something extra." Look for the Olive Oil, Fruit, & Nut Cake, Candied Fruit Cake, and Coffee & Almond Streusel Cake. This chapter also includes a selection of scones and muffins.

Olive Oil, Fruit, & Nut Cake

Serves 8

INGREDIENTS

2 cups self-rising flour
4 tbsp superfine sugar
1/2 cup milk
4 tbsp orange juice

2/3 cup olive oil
2/3 cup mixed dried fruit
1/4 cup pine nuts

1 Grease a 7-inch cake pan with a little butter and line with baking parchment.

2 Sift the flour into a large mixing bowl and stir in the superfine sugar.

3 Make a well in the center of the dry ingredients and pour in the milk and orange juice. Stir the mixture with a wooden spoon, beating in the flour and sugar.

4 Pour in the olive oil, and stir so that all the ingredients are well mixed.

5 Stir the mixed dried fruit and pine nuts into the mixture and spoon into the prepared pan.

6 Bake in a preheated oven at 350°F for about 45 minutes, until the cake is golden and firm to the touch.

7 Leave the cake to cool in the pan for a few minutes before transferring to a wire rack to cool further.

8 Serve the cake warm or cold and cut into slices.

COOK'S TIP

Pine nuts are best known as the flavoring ingredient in the classic Italian pesto, but here they give a delicate, slightly resinous flavor to this cake.

Chocolate & Pear Sponge Cake

Serves 6

INGREDIENTS

3/4 cup butter, softened
1 cup light brown sugar
3 eggs, beaten
1 1/4 cups self-rising flour
2 tbsp unsweetened cocoa

2 tbsp milk
2 small pears, peel, cored, and
  sliced

1 Thoroughly grease an 8-inch loose-bottomed cake pan and line the base with baking parchment.

2 In a bowl, cream together the butter and brown sugar until pale and fluffy.

3 Gradually add the beaten eggs to the creamed mixture, beating well after each addition.

4 Sift the self-rising flour and unsweetened cocoa into the creamed mixture and fold in gently until all of the ingredients are combined.

5 Stir in the milk until well combined, then spoon the mixture into the prepared pan. Level the surface with the back of a spoon or a knife.

6 Place the pear slices on top of the cake mixture, arranging them in a radiating pattern.

7 Bake in a preheated oven at 350°F for about 1 hour, until the cake is just firm to the touch.

8 Let the cake cool in the pan, then transfer to a wire rack until completely cold before serving.

COOK'S TIP

Serve the cake with melted chocolate drizzled over the top for a delicious dessert.

Caraway Madeira

Serves 8

INGREDIENTS

1 cup butter, softened
1 cup light brown sugar
3 eggs, beaten
3 cups self-rising flour
1 tbsp caraway seeds

grated rind of 1 lemon
6 tbsp milk
1 or 2 strips of candied lemon
  peel

1 Grease and line a 2 pound loaf pan.

2 In a bowl, cream together the butter and brown sugar until pale and fluffy.

3 Gradually add the beaten eggs to the creamed mixture, beating well after each addition.

4 Sift the flour into the bowl and gently fold into the creamed mixture.

5 Add the caraway seeds, lemon rind, and the milk and fold in until thoroughly blended.

6 Spoon the mixture into the prepared pan and level the surface with a knife.

7 Bake in a preheated oven at 325°F for 20 minutes.

8 Remove the cake from the oven, place the pieces of candied lemon peel on top of the cake, and return it to the oven for a further 40 minutes, or until the cake is well risen and a knife inserted into the center comes out clean.

9 Let the cake cool in the pan before turning out and transferring to a wire rack until completely cold.

COOK'S TIP

Candied lemon peel is available in the baking section of supermarkets. It should be stored in the freezer for maximum freshness.

Clementine Cake

Serves 8

INGREDIENTS

2 clementines
¾ cup butter, softened
¾ cup superfine sugar
3 eggs, beaten
1½ cups self-rising flour

3 tbsp ground almonds
3 tbsp light cream

GLAZE AND TOPPING:
6 tbsp clementine juice
2 tbsp superfine sugar
3 white sugar cubes, crushed

1 Thoroughly grease a 7-inch round pan and line the base with baking parchment.

2 Pare the rind from the clementines and chop the rind finely. In a bowl, cream together the butter, sugar, and clementine rind until pale and fluffy.

3 Gradually add the beaten eggs to the mixture, beating well after each addition.

4 Gently fold in the self-rising flour, followed by the ground almonds, and the light cream. Spoon the mixture into the prepared pan.

5 Bake in a preheated oven at 350°F for approximately 55–60 minutes, or until a knife inserted into the center of the cake comes out clean. Cool slightly.

6 To make the glaze. Put the clementine juice into a small pan with the superfine sugar. Bring the mixture to a boil and simmer for 5 minutes.

7 Drizzle the glaze over the cake until it has been absorbed, and sprinkle with the crushed sugar cubes.

COOK'S TIP

If you prefer, chop the rind from the clementines in a food processor or blender together with the sugar in step 2. Tip the mixture into a bowl with the butter and begin to cream the mixture.

Candied Fruit Cake

Serves

INGREDIENTS

³/₄ cup butter, softened
³/₄ cup superfine sugar
3 eggs, beaten
1¹/₂ cups self-rising flour,
    sifted

3 tbsp ground rice
finely grated rind of 1 lemon
4 tbsp lemon juice
²/₃ cup candied fruits,
    chopped

confectioners' sugar, for
    dusting (optional)

1 Lightly grease a 7-inch cake pan with butter and line with baking parchment.

2 In a bowl, whisk together the butter and superfine sugar until light and fluffy.

3 Add the beaten eggs, a little at a time, beating well after each addition. Fold in the flour and ground rice.

4 Add the grated lemon rind and juice, then the chopped candied fruits.

Lightly mix all the ingredients together.

5 Spoon the mixture into the prepared pan and level the surface with the back of a spoon or a knife.

6 Bake in a preheated oven at 350°F for 1–1 hour 10 minutes, until well risen or until a knife inserted into the center of the cake comes out clean.

7 Let the cake cool in the pan for 5 minutes, then turn out onto a wire rack and cool completely.

8 Dust well with a little confectioners' sugar, if using, before serving.

COOK'S TIP

Wash and dry the candied fruits before chopping them. This will prevent the fruits sinking to the bottom of the cake during cooking.

White Chocolate & Apricot Squares

Makes 12 bars

INGREDIENTS

1/2 cup butter	1³/4 cups all-purpose flour,	pinch of salt
6 ounces white chocolate,	sifted	1/2 cup chopped ready-to-eat
chopped	1 tsp baking powder	dried apricots
4 eggs		
1/2 cup superfine sugar		

1 Lightly grease a 9-inch square cake pan with a little butter or margarine and line the base of the pan with a sheet of baking parchment.

2 Melt the butter and chocolate in a double boiler. Stir until the mixture is smooth and glossy. Let the mixture cool slightly.

3 Beat the eggs and superfine sugar into the butter and chocolate mixture until well combined.

4 Using a metal spoon, fold in the flour, baking powder, salt, and chopped dried apricots and mix all the ingredients together.

5 Pour the mixture into the prepared cake pan and bake in a preheated oven at 350°F for 25–30 minutes.

6 The center of the cake may not be completely firm when it is removed from the oven, but it will set as it cools. Leave in the pan to cool.

7 When the cake is completely cold turn it out and slice into bars or squares.

VARIATION

Replace the white chocolate with milk or dark chocolate, if you prefer.

Crunchy Fruit Cake

Serves 8–10

INGREDIENTS

$^1/_3$ cup butter, softened
$^1/_2$ cup superfine sugar
2 eggs, beaten
$^1/_3$ cup self-rising flour, sifted

$^2/_3$ cup cornmeal
1 tsp baking powder
$1^2/_3$ cups mixed dried fruit
$^1/_4$ cup pine nuts

grated rind of 1 lemon
4 tbsp lemon juice
2 tbsp milk

1 Thoroughly grease a 7-inch cake pan and line the base with baking parchment.

2 In a bowl, whisk together the butter and sugar until light and fluffy.

3 Whisk in the beaten eggs, a little at a time, whisking well after each addition.

4 Gently fold the sifted flour, baking powder, and cornmeal into the mixture until thoroughly blended.

5 Stir in the mixed dried fruit, pine nuts, grated lemon rind, lemon juice, and milk.

6 Spoon the mixture into the prepared pan and level the surface.

7 Bake in a preheated oven at 350°F for about 1 hour, or until a knife inserted into the center of the cake comes out clean.

8 Leave the cake to cool in the pan before turning out.

VARIATION

To give a more crumbly light fruit cake, omit the cornmeal and use 1$^1/4$ cups self-rising flour instead.

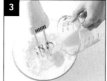

Chocolate Slab Cake with Frosting

Serves 10–12

INGREDIENTS

1 cup butter
3½ ounces dark chocolate,
   chopped
⅔ cup water
2½ cups all-purpose flour
2 tsp baking powder

1⅔ cups light brown sugar
⅔ cup sour cream
2 eggs, beaten

FROSTING:
7 ounces dark chocolate
6 tbsp water
3 tbsp light cream
1 tbsp butter, chilled

1 Thoroughly grease a 13 × 8-inch square cake pan and line the base with baking parchment. In a saucepan, melt the butter and chocolate, together with the water over a low heat, stirring frequently.

2 Sift the flour and baking powder into a mixing bowl and stir in the sugar.

3 Pour the hot chocolate liquid into the bowl and then beat well until all of the ingredients are evenly mixed. Stir in the sour cream, followed by the eggs.

4 Pour the mixture into the prepared pan and bake in a preheated oven at 375°F for 40–45 minutes.

5 Let the cake cool in the pan before turning it out onto a wire rack. Cool completely.

6 To make the frosting, melt the chocolate with the water in a saucepan over a very low heat, stir in the cream, and remove from the heat. Stir in the chilled butter, then pour the frosting over the cooled cake, using a spatula to spread it evenly over the top of the cake.

Chocolate & Almond Torte

Serves 10

INGREDIENTS

8 ounces dark chocolate,
   broken into pieces
3 tbsp water
1 cup light brown sugar
$^3/_4$ cup butter, softened
$^1/_4$ cup ground almonds
3 tbsp self-rising flour

5 eggs, separated
$^1/_4$ cup blanched almonds,
   finely chopped
confectioners' sugar, for
   dusting

heavy cream, to serve
   (optional)

1 Grease a 9-inch loose-bottomed cake pan and base line with baking parchment.

2 In a saucepan set over a very low heat, melt the chocolate with the water, stirring until smooth. Add the sugar and stir until dissolved, taking the pan off the heat to prevent it overheating.

3 Add the butter in small amounts until it has melted into the chocolate.

Remove from the heat and lightly stir in the ground almonds and flour. Add the egg yolks, one at a time, beating well after each addition.

4 In a large mixing bowl, whisk the egg whites until they stand in soft peaks, then fold them into the chocolate mixture with a metal spoon. Stir in the chopped almonds. Pour the mixture into the pan and level the surface with the back of a spoon.

5 Bake in a preheated oven at 350°F for 40–45 minutes, until well risen and firm (the cake will crack on the surface during cooking.)

6 Let the cake cool in the pan for 30–40 minutes, then turn it out onto a wire rack to cool completely. Dust with the top with confectioners' sugar, cut the cake in slices, and serve with heavy cream, if using.

Carrot Cake

Makes 12 bars

INGREDIENTS

1 cup self-rising flour
pinch of salt
1 tsp ground cinnamon
$^3/_4$ cup light brown sugar
2 eggs
scant $^1/_2$ cup sunflower oil
1 cup finely grated carrot

$^1/_3$ cup shredded coconut
$^1/_3$ cup walnuts, chopped
walnut pieces, for decoration

FROSTING:
4 tbsp butter, softened
$^1/_4$ cup full-fat cream cheese
$1^1/_2$ cups confectioners' sugar,
    sifted
1 tsp lemon juice

1 Lightly grease an 8-inch square cake pan and line with baking parchment.

2 Sift the flour, salt, and ground cinnamon into a large bowl and stir in the brown sugar. Add the eggs and oil to the dry ingredients and mix well.

3 Stir in the grated carrot, shredded coconut, and chopped walnuts.

4 Pour the mixture into the prepared cake pan and bake in a preheated oven at 350°F for 20–25 minutes or until it feels just firm to the touch. Cool in the pan.

5 Meanwhile, make the cheese frosting. In a bowl, beat together the butter, full fat soft cheese, confectioners' sugar, and lemon juice until the mixture is fluffy and creamy.

6 Turn the cake out of the pan and cut into 12 bars or slices. Spread with the frosting and then decorate with walnut pieces.

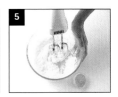

Lemon Syrup Cake

Serves 8

INGREDIENTS

1³/₄ cups all-purpose flour
2 tsp baking powder
1 cup superfine sugar
4 eggs
²/₃ cup sour cream
grated rind 1 large lemon

4 tbsp lemon juice
²/₃ cup sunflower oil

SYRUP:
4 tbsp confectioners' sugar
3 tbsp lemon juice

1 Lightly grease an 8-inch loose-bottomed round cake pan with butter or margarine and line the base with baking parchment.

2 Sift the flour and baking powder into a bowl and stir in the sugar.

3 In a separate bowl, whisk the eggs, sour cream, lemon rind, lemon juice, and oil together.

4 Pour the egg mixture into the dry ingredients and mix well until evenly combined.

5 Pour the mixture into the prepared pan and bake in a preheated oven at 350°F for about 45–60 minutes, until risen and golden brown.

6 Meanwhile, to make the syrup, mix together the confectioners' sugar and lemon juice in a small saucepan. Stir over a low heat until the mixture starts to bubble and turn syrupy.

7 As soon as the cake comes out of the oven prick the surface with a knife, then brush the syrup over the top. Let the cake cool completely in the pan before turning out and serving.

COOK'S TIP

Pricking the surface of the hot cake ensures that the syrup seeps right into the cake.

Orange Kugelhopf Cake

Serves 6–8

INGREDIENTS

1 cup butter, softened
1 cup superfine sugar
4 eggs, separated
3 3/4 cups all-purpose flour
3 tsp baking powder
pinch of salt
1 1/4 cups fresh orange juice

1 tbsp orange flower water
1 tsp grated orange rind

SYRUP:
3/4 cup orange juice
1 cup sugar

1 Grease and flour a 10-inch kugelhopf pan or deep ring mold.

2 Cream together the butter and superfine sugar until light and fluffy. Add the egg yolks, one at a time, whisking well after each addition.

3 Sift together the flour, salt, and baking powder. Fold the dry ingredients and the orange juice alternately into the creamed mixture with a metal spoon.

Stir in the orange flower water and orange rind.

4 Whisk the egg whites until they reach the soft peak stage and fold them into the mixture.

5 Pour into the prepared mold and bake in a preheated oven at 350°F for 50–55 minutes, or until a knife inserted into center of the cake comes out clean.

6 In a saucepan, bring the orange juice and

sugar to a boil, and simmer for 5 minutes until the sugar has dissolved.

7 Remove the cake from the oven and cool in the pan for 10 minutes. Prick the top of the cake with a knife and brush over half of the syrup. Let the cake cool for another 10 minutes. Invert the cake onto a wire rack placed over a deep plate and brush the syrup over the cake until it is entirely covered. Serve.

Coconut Cake

Serves 6–8

INGREDIENTS

2 cups self-rising flour
pinch of salt
$^{1}/_{2}$ cup butter, cut into small
    pieces
$^{1}/_{2}$ cup raw crystal sugar

1 cup shredded coconut, plus
    extra for sprinkling
2 eggs, beaten
4 tbsp milk

1 Grease a 2-pound loaf pan and line the base with baking parchment.

2 Sift the flour and salt into a mixing bowl and rub in the butter with your fingertips until the mixture resembles fine breadcrumbs.

3 Stir in the sugar, coconut, eggs, and milk and mix to a soft dropping consistency.

4 Spoon the mixture into the prepared pan and level the surface with the back of a spoon. Bake in a preheated oven at 325°F for 30 minutes.

5 Remove the cake from the oven and sprinkle with the reserved coconut. Return the cake to the oven and cook for another 30 minutes, until well risen with a light golden brown color, and a knife inserted into the center comes out clean.

6 Let the cake cool in the pan before turning out and transferring to a wire rack to cool completely before serving.

COOK'S TIP

The flavor of this cake is enhanced by storing it in a cool dry place for a few days before eating.

Apple Cake with Cider

Makes an 8-inch cake

INGREDIENTS

2 cups self-rising flour
1 tsp baking powder
1/3 cup butter, cut into small
    pieces
1/3 cup superfine sugar
3 1/2 cups chopped dried apple
5 tbsp raisins

2/3 cup sweet cider
1 egg, beaten
1 cup raspberries

1 Thoroughly grease an 8-inch cake pan with butter or margarine and line with baking parchment.

2 Sift the flour and baking powder into a bowl and rub in the butter with your fingers until the mixture resembles fine breadcrumbs.

3 Stir in the superfine sugar, chopped dried apple, and the raisins and mix until well combined

4 Pour in the sweet cider and egg and mix together until thoroughly blended. Stir in the raspberries very gently so they do not break up.

5 Pour the mixture into the prepared cake pan.

6 Bake in a preheated oven at 375°F for about 40 minutes, until well risen and a light golden color.

7 Let the cake cool in the pan, then turn out onto a wire rack. Leave until completely cold before serving. Cut into slices to serve.

VARIATION

If you don't want to use cider, replace it with clear apple juice, if you prefer.

Spiced Apple Ring

Serves 8

INGREDIENTS

³/₄ cup butter, softened	1 tsp ground cinnamon	2 tbsp apple juice or milk
³/₄ cup superfine sugar	1 tsp apple pie spice	¹/₄ cup slivered almonds
3 eggs, beaten	2 eating apples, cored and	
1¹/₂ cups self-rising flour	grated	

1 Lightly grease a 10-inch ovenproof ring mold.

2 In a mixing bowl, cream together the butter and sugar until light and fluffy. Gradually add the beaten eggs, beating well after each addition, until well combined.

3 Sift the flour and spices, then carefully fold them into the creamed mixture.

4 Stir in the grated apples and the apple juice or milk and mix together to form a soft dropping consistency.

5 Sprinkle the slivered almonds around the base of the mold and spoon the cake mixture on top. Level the surface with the back of the spoon.

6 Bake in a preheated oven at 350°F for about 30 minutes, until well risen and a knife inserted into the center comes out clean.

7 Let the cake cool in the pan for about 10 minutes before turning out and transferring to a wire rack to cool completely. Serve the spiced apple ring cut into slices.

COOK'S TIP

This cake can also be made in a 7-inch round cake pan if you do not have an ovenproof ring mold.

Marbled Chocolate Cake

Serves 8

INGREDIENTS

³/₄ cup butter, softened
³/₄ cup superfine sugar
3 eggs, beaten

1¹/₄ cups self-rising flour,
sifted
¹/₄ cup unsweetened cocoa,
sifted

5–6 tbsp orange juice
grated rind of 1 orange

1 Lightly grease a 10-inch ovenproof ring mold.

2 In a mixing bowl, cream together the butter and sugar with an electric mixer for about 5 minutes.

3 Add the beaten egg, a little at a time, beating well after each addition.

4 Using a metal spoon, carefully fold the flour into the creamed mixture. Spoon half of the mixture into a separate mixing bowl.

5 Fold the cocoa and half of the orange juice into one bowl and mix gently.

6 Fold the orange rind and remaining orange juice into the other bowl and mix gently.

7 Place spoonfuls of each of the mixtures alternately into the mold, then drag a knife through the mixture to create a marbled effect.

8 Bake in a preheated oven at 350°F for 30–35 minutes, until well

risen and a knife inserted into the center comes out clean.

9 Let the cake cool in the mold before turning out onto a wire rack. Serve the cake cut into slices.

VARIATION

For a richer chocolate flavor, add ¹/₃ cup chocolate chips to the cocoa mixture.

Coffee & Almond Streusel Cake

Serves 8

INGREDIENTS

1¼ cups all-purpose flour
1 tbsp baking powder
⅓ cup superfine sugar
⅔ cup milk
2 eggs

½ cup butter, melted and
    cooled
2 tbsp instant coffee mixed
    with 1 tbsp boiling water
⅓ cup almonds, chopped
confectioners' sugar, for
    dusting

TOPPING:
½ cup self-rising flour
⅓ cup raw crystal sugar
2 tbsp butter, cut into
    small pieces
1 tsp apple pie spice
1 tbsp water

1 Thoroughly grease a 9-inch loose-bottomed round cake pan and line with baking parchment. Sift together the flour and baking powder into a large mixing bowl, then stir in the superfine sugar.

2 Whisk the milk, eggs, butter, and coffee mixture together and pour onto the dry ingredients. Add the chopped almonds and mix lightly together. Spoon the mixture into the pan.

3 To make the topping, mix the flour and raw crystal sugar together in a separate bowl. Rub in the butter with your fingers until the mixture is crumbly. Sprinkle in the apple pie spice and the water and bring the mixture together in loose crumbs. Sprinkle the topping over the cake mixture.

4 Bake in a preheated oven at 375°F for 50 minutes–1 hour. Cover loosely with foil if the topping starts to brown too quickly. Let the cake cool in the pan, then turn out to cool completely. Dust with a little confectioners' sugar just before serving.

Sugar-free Fruit Cake

Serves 8–10

INGREDIENTS

3 cups all-purpose flour
2 tsp baking powder
1 tsp apple pie spice
1/2 cup butter, cut into small pieces
3/4 cup chopped ready-to-eat dried apricots

1/2 cup pitted chopped dates
1/2 cup candied cherries, chopped
2/3 cup raisins
1/2 cup milk
2 eggs, beaten
grated rind of 1 orange

5–6 tbsp orange juice
3 tbsp clear honey

1 Grease an 8-inch round cake pan and line the base with baking parchment.

2 Sift the flour, baking powder, and apple pie spice into a large mixing bowl.

3 Rub in the butter with your fingers until the mixture resembles fine breadcrumbs.

4 Carefully stir in the chopped apricots, dates, candied cherries, and raisins with the milk, beaten eggs, grated orange rind, and orange juice and mix well together.

5 Stir in the honey and mix everything together to a soft dropping consistency. Spoon the mixture into the prepared cake pan and level the surface.

6 Bake in a preheated oven at 350°F for 1 hour until a knife inserted into the center of the cake comes out clean.

7 Let the cake cool in the pan before turning out.

VARIATION

For a fruity alternative, replace the honey with 1 mashed ripe banana, if you prefer.

Almond Cake

Serves 8

INGREDIENTS

1/3 cup soft margarine	1 tsp baking powder	SYRUP:
3 tbsp light brown sugar	4 tbsp milk	2/3 cup clear honey
2 eggs	2 tbsp clear honey	2 tbsp lemon juice
1 1/2 cups self-rising flour	1/2 cup slivered almonds	

1 Thoroughly grease a 7-inch round cake pan and line with baking parchment.

2 Place the margarine, brown sugar, eggs, flour, baking powder, milk, and honey in a large mixing bowl and beat well with a wooden spoon for about 1 minute, until all of the ingredients are thoroughly mixed together.

3 Spoon into the prepared pan, level the surface, and sprinkle with the almonds.

4 Bake the mixture in a preheated oven at 350°F for 50 minutes, or until the cake is well risen.

5 To make the syrup, combine the honey and lemon juice in a small pan and simmer for 5 minutes, or until the syrup starts to coat the back of a spoon.

6 As soon as the cake comes out of the oven, pour the syrup on top, allowing it to seep into the middle of the cake.

7 Let the cake cool for at least 2 hours before slicing.

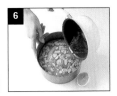

Gingerbread

Makes 12 bars

INGREDIENTS

²/₃ cup butter
1 cup light brown sugar
2 tbsp molasses
2 cups all-purpose flour

1 tsp baking powder
2 tsp baking soda
2 tsp ground ginger
²/₃ cup milk

1 egg, beaten
2 eating apples, peeled,
    chopped, and coated with
    1 tbsp lemon juice

1 Thoroughly grease a 9-inch square cake pan with butter or margarine and line with baking parchment.

2 Melt the butter, sugar, and molasses in a saucepan over a low heat and let the mixture cool.

3 Sift the flour, baking powder, soda, and ginger into a mixing bowl.

4 Stir in the milk, beaten egg, and cooled butter, sugar, and molasses

mixture, followed by the chopped apples coated with the lemon juice.

5 Mix everything together gently, then pour the mixture into the prepared pan.

6 Bake in a preheated oven at 325°F for 30–35 minutes, until the cake has risen and a knife inserted into the center comes out clean.

7 Let the cake cool in the pan before turning out

onto a wire rack and cutting into 12 bars.

VARIATION

If you enjoy the flavor of ginger, try adding 2 tablespoons finely chopped preserved ginger to the mixture in step 3.

Apple Shortcakes

Serves 8

INGREDIENTS

1¹/4 cups all-purpose flour
¹/2 tsp salt
1 tsp baking powder
1 tbsp superfine sugar
1 tbsp butter, cut into
    small pieces
¹/4 cup milk

confectioners' sugar, for
    dusting

FILLING:
3 eating apples, peeled, cored,
    and sliced
¹/2 cup superfine sugar
1 tbsp lemon juice

1 tsp ground cinnamon
1¹/3 cups water
²/3 cup heavy cream, whipped
    lightly

1 Lightly grease a cookie sheet.

2 Sift together the flour, salt, and baking powder into a mixing bowl. Stir in the sugar, then rub in the butter until the mixture resembles fine breadcrumbs. Pour in the milk and mix everything to a soft dough.

3 Knead the dough lightly, then roll out to a thickness of ¹/2 inch.

Stamp out 4 rounds, using a 2-inch cutter. Transfer the rounds to the prepared cookie sheet. Bake in a preheated oven at 425°F for about 15 minutes, until the shortcakes are well risen and lightly browned. Let the shortcakes cool.

4 To make the filling, place the apple slices, sugar, lemon juice, and cinnamon in a saucepan. Add the water, bring to a boil, and simmer uncovered

for 5–10 minutes, until the apples are tender. Cool a little, then remove the apples from the pan.

5 To serve, split the shortcakes in half. Place each bottom half on an individual serving plate and spoon on a quarter of the apple slices, then the cream. Place the other half of the shortcake on top. Serve dusted with confectioners' sugar, if desired.

Rich Scones

Makes 8

INGREDIENTS

2 cups self-rising flour	$^1/_3$ cup butter, cut into small	1 egg, beaten
1 tbsp superfine sugar	pieces	2 tbsp molasses
pinch of salt	1 eating apple, peeled, cored,	5 tbsp milk
	and chopped	

1 Lightly grease a cookie sheet.

2 Sift the flour, sugar, and salt into a mixing bowl.

3 Rub in the butter with your fingers until the mixture resembles fine breadcrumbs.

4 Stir the chopped apple into the mixture until combined.

5 Mix the beaten egg, molasses, and milk together. Add to the dry ingredients to form a soft dough.

6 On a lightly floured kitchen counter, roll out the dough to a thickness of $^3/_4$ inch and cut out 8 scones, using a 2-inch plain pastry cutter.

7 Arrange the scones on the prepared cookie sheet and bake in a preheated oven at 425°F for 8–10 minutes.

8 Transfer the scones to a wire rack and cool slightly before serving.

9 Serve split in half and spread with butter.

COOK'S TIP

These scones can be frozen, but are best defrosted and eaten within 1 month.

Cherry Scones

Makes 8

INGREDIENTS

2 cups self-rising flour
1 tbsp superfine sugar
pinch of salt

$^1/_3$ cup butter, cut into small
  pieces
3 tbsp candied cherries,
  chopped

3 tbsp golden raisins
1 egg, beaten
$^1/_4$ cup milk

1 Lightly grease a cookie sheet with a little butter.

2 Sift together the flour, sugar, and salt into a mixing bowl and rub in the butter with your fingers until the scone mixture resembles breadcrumbs.

3 Stir in the candied cherries and golden raisins. Add the beaten egg.

4 Reserve 1 tablespoon of the milk for glazing, then add the remainder to the mixture. Mix together to form a soft dough.

5 On a lightly floured surface, roll out the dough to a thickness of $^3/_4$ inch and cut out 8 scones, using a 2-inch plain pastry cutter.

6 Place the scones on the cookie sheet and brush with the reserved milk.

7 Bake in a preheated oven at 425°F for 8–10 minutes, or until the scones are golden brown.

8 Let cool slightly on a wire rack, then serve split and buttered.

COOK'S TIP

These scones will freeze very successfully, but they are best defrosted and eaten within 1 month.

Cranberry Muffins

Makes 18

INGREDIENTS

2 cups all-purpose flour
2 tsp baking powder
1/2 tsp salt

3 tbsp superfine sugar
4 tbsp butter, melted
2 eggs, beaten

3/4 cup milk
1 cup fresh cranberries
2 tbsp freshly grated
Parmesan cheese

1 Lightly grease 2 muffin pans with a little butter

2 Sift the flour, baking powder, and salt into a mixing bowl. Stir in the superfine sugar.

3 In a separate bowl, mix the butter, beaten eggs, and milk together, then pour into the bowl of dry ingredients.

4 Mix lightly together until all of the ingredients are evenly combined, then stir in the fresh cranberries.

5 Divide the mixture between the prepared pans.

6 Sprinkle the grated Parmesan cheese over the top of each muffin mixture.

7 Bake in a preheated oven at 400°F for about 20 minutes, or until the cranberry muffins are well risen and a golden brown color.

8 Let the muffins cool slightly in the pans. Transfer the muffins to a

wire rack and cool completely before serving.

VARIATION

For a sweet alternative to this recipe, replace the Parmesan cheese with raw crystal sugar in step 5, if you prefer.

Cookies

Nothing can compare with a homemade cookie for bringing a touch of pleasure to a coffee break or tea-time. This selection of delicious cookies and after-dinner treats will tantalize your taste buds and keep you coming back for more.

Tempting cookies like Citrus Crescents, Chocolate Chip Cookies, and Gingernuts are quick and easy to make. You can easily vary the finished shape of Vanilla Hearts, Caraway Cookies, and Lemon Jumbles if you have a favorite cookie cutter! The possibilities for inventiveness when making cookies are endless.

For cookie making, you need the best ingredients: nuts should be as fresh as possible, use good quality dark and white chocolate, sugars should be unrefined pure cane sugars, and you will discover that the best cookies are made with butter.

Always cool cookies on a wire rack and then store them in an airtight container to keep them fresh.

Spiced Cookies

Makes about 24

INGREDIENTS

³/4 cup sweet butter
1 cup dark brown sugar
2 cups all-purpose flour
pinch of salt

¹/2 tsp baking soda
1 tsp ground cinnamon
¹/2 tsp ground coriander

¹/2 tsp ground nutmeg
¹/4 tsp ground cloves
2 tbsp dark rum

1 Lightly grease 2 cookie sheets with a little butter.

2 In a large mixing bowl, cream together the butter and dark brown sugar and beat until light and fluffy.

3 Sift the flour, salt, baking soda, cinnamon, coriander, nutmeg, and cloves into the creamed mixture and mix well until all the ingredients are thoroughly combined.

4 Stir the dark rum into the creamed mixture.

5 Using 2 teaspoons, place small mounds of the mixture onto the cookie sheets 3 inches apart to allow for spreading during cooking. Flatten each mound slightly with the back of a spoon.

6 Bake in a preheated oven at 350°F for about 10 minutes, or until golden.

7 Transfer the cookies to wire racks and let them cool and crispen before serving.

COOK'S TIP

Use the back of a fork to flatten the cookies slightly before baking.

Cinnamon & Sunflower Squares

Makes 12

INGREDIENTS

1 cup butter, softened	2 cups self-rising flour	1 tbsp ground cinnamon
1 1/4 cups superfine sugar	1/2 tsp baking soda	2/3 cup sour cream
3 eggs, beaten		2/3 cup sunflower seeds

1 Grease a 9-inch square cake pan with a little butter and line the base with baking parchment.

2 Put the butter and superfine sugar into a large mixing bowl and cream them together until the mixture becomes light and fluffy.

3 Gradually add the beaten eggs to the mixture, beating well after each addition.

4 Sift the flour, baking soda, and ground cinnamon into the creamed mixture and fold in gently, using a metal spoon.

5 Spoon in the sour cream and sunflower seeds and gently mix together until well combined.

6 Spoon the mixture into the prepared cake pan and level the surface with the back of a spoon or a knife.

7 Bake in a preheated oven at 350°F for about 45 minutes, or until the mixture is firm to the touch when pressed.

8 Loosen the edges with a round-bladed knife, then turn out onto a wire rack to cool completely. Slice into 12 squares and serve.

COOK'S TIP

These moist squares will freeze well and keep for up to 1 month.

Gingernuts

Makes 30

INGREDIENTS

3 cups self-rising flour
pinch of salt
1 cup superfine sugar

1 tbsp ground ginger
1 tsp baking soda
1/2 cup butter

1/4 cup light corn syrup
1 egg, beaten
1 tsp grated orange rind

1 Lightly grease several cookie sheets with butter or margarine.

2 Sift the flour, salt, sugar, ginger, and baking soda into a large mixing bowl.

3 Heat the butter and light corn syrup together in a saucepan over a very low heat until the butter has completely melted.

4 Let the butter mixture cool slightly, then pour it onto the dry ingredients.

5 Add the egg and orange rind and mix thoroughly.

6 Using your hands, carefully shape the dough into 30 even-size balls.

7 Place the balls on the prepared cookie sheets, spacing them well apart to allow for spreading during cooking, then flatten them slightly with your fingers.

8 Bake in a preheated oven at 325°F for 15–20 minutes, then transfer the gingernuts to a wire rack to cool before serving.

VARIATION

If you like your gingernuts crunchy, bake them in the oven for a few minutes longer.

Caraway Cookies

Makes about 36

INGREDIENTS

2 cups all-purpose flour
pinch of salt
$1/3$ cup butter, cut into small
   pieces

$1^{1}/4$ cups superfine sugar
1 egg, beaten

2 tbsp caraway seeds
raw crystal sugar, for
   sprinkling (optional)

1 Lightly grease several cookie sheets with butter.

2 Sift the flour and salt into a mixing bowl. Rub in the butter with your fingertips until the mixture resembles fine breadcrumbs. Stir in the superfine sugar.

3 Reserve 1 tablespoon of the beaten egg for brushing the cookies and add the rest to the mixture, together with the caraway seeds. Bring together to form a soft dough.

4 On a lightly floured surface, roll out the cookie dough thinly and then cut out about 36 rounds with a $2^{1}/2$-inch cookie cutter.

5 Transfer the cookies to the prepared cookie sheets, brush with the reserved beaten egg, and sprinkle with a little raw crystal sugar.

6 Bake in a preheated oven at 325°F for 10–15 minutes, until the cookies are crisp and lightly golden in color.

7 Let the cookies cool on a wire rack and store in an airtight container.

VARIATION

Caraway seeds have a nutty, delicate anise flavor. If you don't like their flavor, replace the caraway seeds with the milder-flavored poppy seeds.

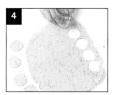

Peanut Butter Cookies

Makes 20

INGREDIENTS

$^1/_2$ cup butter, softened
$^1/_2$ cup chunky peanut butter
1 cup sugar

1 egg, lightly beaten
1 $^1/_4$ cups all-purpose flour
$^1/_2$ tsp baking powder

pinch of salt
$^3/_4$ cup unsalted natural
    peanuts, chopped

1 Lightly grease 2 cookie sheets.

2 In a large mixing bowl, beat together the butter and peanut butter.

3 Gradually add the sugar and beat well.

4 Add the beaten egg, a little at a time, beating until it is thoroughly combined.

5 Sift the flour, baking powder, and salt into the peanut butter mixture.

6 Add the peanuts and bring all of the ingredients together to form a soft dough. Wrap and chill for about 30 minutes.

7 Form the dough into 20 balls and place them onto the prepared cookie sheets about 2 inches apart to allow for spreading. Flatten them slightly with a fork.

8 Bake in a preheated oven at 375°F for 15 minutes, until a golden brown color. Transfer the cookies to a wire rack and cool slightly before serving.

COOK'S TIP

For a crunchy bite and sparkling appearance, sprinkle the cookies with raw crystal sugar just before they are baked.

Hazelnut Squares

Makes 16

INGREDIENTS

1¼ cups all-purpose flour
pinch of salt
1 tsp baking powder

⅓ cup butter, cut into small
    pieces
1 cup light brown sugar
1 egg, beaten
4 tbsp milk

1 cup hazelnuts, halved
raw crystal sugar, for
    sprinkling (optional)

1 Grease a 9-inch square cake pan and line the base with baking parchment.

2 Sift the flour, salt, and baking powder into a large mixing bowl.

3 Rub in the butter with your fingers until the mixture resembles fine breadcrumbs. Stir in the brown sugar.

4 Add the egg, milk, and nuts to the mixture and stir well until all the ingredients are thoroughly combined.

5 Spoon the mixture into the prepared cake pan and level the surface. Sprinkle with raw crystal sugar, if using.

6 Bake in a preheated oven at 350°F for about 25 minutes, or until firm to the touch.

7 Cool slightly for 10 minutes, loosen the edges with a round-bladed knife, and turn out onto a wire rack to cool further. Cut into squares.

VARIATION

For a coffee time cookie, replace the milk with the same amount of cold strong black coffee—the stronger the better!

Coconut Cookies

Makes 16 squares

INGREDIENTS

1 cup butter
1 1/3 cups raw crystal sugar

2 tbsp light corn syrup
3 1/2 cups dried oats
1 cup shredded coconut

1/3 cup candied cherries,
   chopped

1 Lightly grease a 12 × 9-inch cookie sheet with butter..

2 Heat the butter, raw crystal sugar, and light corn syrup in a large saucepan over a low heat until just melted.

3 Stir in the oats, shredded coconut, and candied cherries and mix well until all the ingredients are combined.

4 Spread the mixture onto the cookie sheet and press down with the back of a spatula to make a smooth surface.

5 Bake in a preheated oven at 325°F for about 30 minutes.

6 Remove the cookies from the oven and let them cool slightly on the cookie sheet for about 10 minutes.

7 Cut the mixture into even-sized rectangles using a sharp knife.

8 Carefully transfer the coconut cookies to a wire rack and cool completely.

COOK'S TIP

These cookies are best stored in an airtight container and eaten within 1 week. They can also be frozen for up to 1 month.

Oat & Raisin Cookies

Makes 10

INGREDIENTS

4 tbsp butter	$1/2$ cup all-purpose flour	2 cups oats
$1/2$ cup superfine sugar	$1/2$ tsp salt	$3/4$ cup raisins
1 egg, beaten	$1/2$ tsp baking powder	2 tbsp sesame seeds

1 Lightly grease 2 cookie sheets.

2 In a large mixing bowl, cream together the butter and sugar until light and fluffy.

3 Add the beaten egg gradually and beat until well combined.

4 Sift the flour, salt and baking powder into the creamed mixture. Mix well.

5 Add the oats, raisins, and sesame seeds and mix together thoroughly.

6 Place spoonfuls of the mixture well apart (to allow for spreading during baking) on the prepared cookie sheets and flatten them slightly with the back of a spoon.

7 Bake the cookies in a preheated oven at 350°F for 15 minutes.

8 Let the cookies cool slightly on the cookie sheets.

9 Transfer the cookies to a wire rack and cool completely before serving.

VARIATION

Substitute chopped ready-to-eat dried apricots for the raisins, if you prefer.

COOK'S TIP

To enjoy these cookies at their best, store them in an airtight container.

Rosemary Cookies

Makes about 25

INGREDIENTS

2 tbsp butter, softened
4 tbsp superfine sugar
grated rind of 1 lemon
4 tbsp lemon juice

1 egg, separated
2 tsp finely chopped fresh
  rosemary
1³/4 cups all-purpose flour,
  sifted

superfine sugar, for sprinkling
(optional)

1 Lightly grease 2 cookie sheets with butter or margarine.

2 In a large mixing bowl, cream together the butter and sugar until pale and fluffy.

3 Add the lemon rind and juice, then the egg yolk, and beat until all the ingredients are thoroughly combined. Stir in the chopped fresh rosemary.

4 Add the sifted flour, mixing well until a soft dough is formed. Wrap and chill in the refrigerator for 30 minutes.

5 On a lightly floured surface, roll out the dough thinly and stamp out about 25 cookies with a 2½-inch cookie cutter. Arrange the dough on the prepared cookie sheets.

6 In a small bowl, lightly beat the egg white. Gently brush the egg white over the surface of each cookie, then sprinkle with a little superfine sugar, if desired.

7 Bake the cookies in a preheated oven at 350°F for about 15 minutes.

8 Transfer the cookies to a wire rack and cool completely before serving.

VARIATION

In place of the fresh rosemary, use 1½ teaspoons of dried rosemary, if you prefer.

Citrus Crescents

Makes about 25

INGREDIENTS

1/3 cup butter, softened	1 3/4 cups all-purpose flour	grated rind of 1 lime
1/3 cup superfine sugar	grated rind of 1 orange	2–3 tbsp orange juice
1 egg, separated	grated rind of 1 lemon	superfine sugar, for sprinkling (optional)

1 Lightly grease 2 cookie sheets.

2 In a mixing bowl, cream together the butter and sugar until light and fluffy, then gradually pour in the egg yolk, beating well after each addition.

3 Sift the flour into the creamed mixture and mix until evenly combined. Add the orange, lemon, and lime rinds to the mixture with enough of the orange juice to make a soft dough.

4 Roll out the dough on a lightly floured surface. Stamp out cookies using a 3-inch cookie cutter. Make crescent shapes by cutting away a quarter of each cookie. Re-roll the pastry trimmings to make about 25 crescents.

5 Prick the surface of each crescent with a fork. Place the crescents onto the cookie sheets.

6 Lightly beat the egg white in a small bowl and gently brush it over the cookies. Dust the cookies with extra superfine sugar, if using.

7 Bake in a preheated oven at 400°F for 12–15 minutes. Transfer the cookies to a wire rack and cool slightly before serving.

COOK'S TIP

Store the citrus crescents in an airtight container or freeze them for up to 1 month.

Lemon Jumbles

Makes about 50

INGREDIENTS

¹/₃ cup butter, softened	1 egg, beaten	1 tsp baking powder
¹/₂ cup superfine sugar	4 tbsp lemon juice	1 tbsp milk
grated rind of 1 lemon	3 cups all-purpose flour	confectioners' sugar, for dredging

1 Lightly grease several cookie sheets with butter.

2 In a mixing bowl, cream together the butter, superfine sugar, and lemon rind until pale and fluffy.

3 Add the beaten egg and lemon juice a little at a time, beating well after each addition.

4 Sift the flour and baking powder into the creamed mixture and blend together until well combined. Add the milk, mixing to form a dough.

5 Turn the dough out onto a lightly floured surface and divide into about 50 equal-size pieces.

6 Roll each piece into a sausage shape with your hands and twist in the middle to make an "S" shape.

7 Place the shapes on the cookie sheets and bake in a preheated oven at 325°F for 15–20 minutes. Cool completely on a wire rack and dredge with confectioners' sugar before serving.

VARIATION

If you prefer, shape the dough into other shapes—letters of the alphabet or geometric shapes—or just make into round cookies.

Chocolate & Lemon Pinwheels

Makes about 40

INGREDIENTS

³/₄ cup butter, softened	1 egg, beaten	1 ounce dark chocolate,
1¹/₃ cups superfine sugar	3 cups all-purpose flour	melted and cooled slightly
		grated rind of 1 lemon

1 Grease and flour several cookie sheets.

2 In a large mixing bowl, cream together the butter and sugar until light and fluffy.

3 Gradually add the beaten egg to the creamed mixture, beating well after each addition.

4 Sift the flour into the creamed mixture and mix until a soft dough forms.

5 Transfer half of the dough to another bowl

and beat in the cooled melted chocolate.

6 Stir the grated lemon rind into the other half of the plain dough.

7 On a lightly floured surface, roll out the 2 pieces of dough to form rectangles of the same size.

8 Lay the lemon dough on top of the chocolate dough. Roll up the dough tightly into a sausage shape, using a sheet of baking parchment to guide you. Let the dough chill slightly in the refrigerator.

9 Cut the roll into about 40 slices, place them on the cookie sheets, and bake in a preheated oven at 375°F for 10–12 minutes, or until lightly golden. Transfer the pinwheels to a wire rack and cool completely before serving.

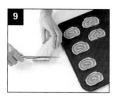

White Chocolate Cookies

Makes 24

INGREDIENTS

1/2 cup butter, softened	1 3/4 cups self-rising flour	4 1/2 ounces white chocolate,
3/4 cup light brown sugar	pinch of salt	roughly chopped
1 egg, beaten		1/2 cup chopped Brazil nuts

1 Lightly grease several cookie sheets.

2 In a large mixing bowl, cream together the butter and sugar until light and fluffy.

3 Gradually add the beaten egg to the creamed mixture, beating well after each addition.

4 Sift the flour and salt into the creamed mixture and blend well.

5 Stir in the chocolate chunks and Brazil nuts.

6 Place heaping teaspoons of the white chocolate mixture onto the prepared cookie sheets. Space them well apart as the cookies will spread considerably during cooking.

7 Bake in a preheated oven at 375°F for 10–12 minutes, or until the cookies are a light golden brown color.

8 Transfer the cookies to wire racks and set aside until completely cold and crisp before serving.

VARIATION

Use dark or milk chocolate instead of white chocolate, if you prefer.

Shortbread Fantails

Makes 8

INGREDIENTS

½ cup butter, softened	2 cups all-purpose flour	superfine sugar, for sprinkling
¼ cup sugar	pinch of salt	
¼ cup confectioners' sugar	2 tsp orange flower water	

1 Lightly grease an 8-inch shallow round cake pan with a little butter.

2 In a large mixing bowl, cream together the butter, the sugar, and the confectioners' sugar until the mixture is light and fluffy.

3 Sift the flour and salt into the creamed mixture. Add the orange flower water and bring everything together to form a soft dough.

4 On a lightly floured surface, roll out the dough to an 8-inch round and place in the pan. Prick the dough well and score into 8 triangles with a round-bladed knife.

5 Bake in a preheated oven at 300°F for 30–35 minutes, or until the cookie is crisp and pale golden in color.

6 Sprinkle with a little superfine sugar, then cut along the marked lines to make the fantails.

7 Let the shortbread cool completely before removing the pieces from the pan. Store in an airtight container.

COOK'S TIP

For a crunchy addition, sprinkle 2 tablespoons of chopped mixed nuts over the top of the fantails before baking.

Millionaire's Shortbread

Makes 12 bars

INGREDIENTS

1¹/₂ cups all-purpose flour
¹/₂ cup butter, cut into small
pieces

3 tbsp light brown sugar,
sifted

TOPPING:
4 tbsp butter
3 tbsp light brown sugar

14 ounce can condensed milk
5¹/₂ ounces milk chocolate

1 Thoroughly grease a 9-inch square cake pan.

2 Sift the flour into a bowl and rub in the butter with your fingertips until the mixture resembles fine breadcrumbs. Add the sugar and mix to form a firm dough.

3 Press the dough into the prepared pan and prick with a fork.

4 Bake in a preheated oven at 375°F for 20 minutes, until lightly golden. Cool completely in the pan.

5 To make the topping, place the butter, sugar, and condensed milk in a nonstick saucepan and cook over a gentle heat, stirring constantly, until the mixture comes to a boil.

6 Reduce the heat and cook for 4–5 minutes, until the caramel is pale golden and thick and is coming away from the sides of the pan. Pour over the shortbread base and let cool.

7 When the caramel topping is firm, melt the milk chocolate in a double boiler. Spread the melted chocolate over the topping, set aside in a cool place, then cut the shortbread into squares or bars to serve.

Vanilla Hearts

Makes about 16

INGREDIENTS

2 cups all-purpose flour
$2/3$ cup butter, cut into small
    pieces

$1/2$ cup superfine sugar
1 tsp vanilla extract

superfine sugar, for dusting

1 Lightly grease a cookie sheet with a little butter.

2 Sift the flour into a large mixing bowl and rub in the butter with your fingers until the mixture is well combined and resembles fine breadcrumbs.

3 Stir in the superfine sugar and vanilla extract and bring the mixture together to make a firm dough.

4 On a lightly floured kitchen surface, roll out the dough to a thickness of about 1 inch. Stamp out 12 heart shapes with a heart-shaped cookie cutter measuring about 2 inches across and 1 inch deep.

5 Arrange the hearts on the prepared cookie sheet. Bake in a preheated oven at 350°F for about 15–20 minutes, until the hearts are a light golden color.

6 Transfer the hearts to a wire rack. Let the cookies cool slightly before serving. Dust the vanilla hearts with a little superfine sugar, if desired.

COOK'S TIP

Place a fresh vanilla bean in your superfine sugar and keep it in a storage jar for several weeks to give the sugar a delicious vanilla flavor.

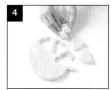

Rock Drops

Makes 8

INGREDIENTS

1³/4 cups all-purpose flour
2 tsp baking powder
1/3 cup butter, cut into small
  pieces
	1/3 cup raw crystal sugar
	1/2 cup golden raisins
		2 tbsp candied cherries,
		  finely chopped
		1 egg, beaten
		2 tbsp milk

1 Lightly grease a cookie sheet with a little butter or margarine.

2 Sift the flour and baking powder into a large mixing bowl. Rub in the butter with your fingers until well combined and the mixture resembles breadcrumbs.

3 Stir in the raw crystal sugar, golden raisins, and chopped candied cherries, combining all the ingredients thoroughly.

4 Add the beaten egg and the milk to the mixture and mix to form a soft dough.

5 Spoon 8 mounds of the mixture onto the cookie sheet, spacing them well apart as they will spread while they are cooking.

6 Bake in a preheated oven at 400°F for 15–20 minutes, until firm to the touch when pressed with a finger.

7 Remove the rock drops from the cookie sheet. You can either serve them piping hot from the oven or transfer them to a wire rack and let cool before serving.

COOK'S TIP

For convenience, prepare the dry ingredients in advance and just before cooking stir in the liquid.

Chocolate Chip Brownies

Makes 12

INGREDIENTS

5¹/2 ounces dark chocolate,
broken into pieces
1 cup butter, softened
2 cups self-rising flour

¹/2 cup superfine sugar
4 eggs, beaten
³/4 cup chopped pistachio nuts

3¹/2 ounces white chocolate,
roughly chopped
confectioners' sugar, for
dusting

1 Lightly grease a 9-inch baking pan and line with wax paper.

2 Melt the dark chocolate and butter in a double boiler. Leave to cool slightly.

3 Sift the flour into a separate mixing bowl and stir in the superfine sugar.

4 Stir the eggs into the melted chocolate mixture, then pour this mixture into the flour and sugar mixture, beating well. Stir in the pistachio nuts and white chocolate, then pour the mixture into the pan, spreading it evenly into the corners.

5 Bake in a preheated oven at 350° for 30–35 minutes, until firm to the touch. Cool in the pan for about 20 minutes, then turn out onto a wire rack to cool further.

6 Dust the surface of the cookies with a little confectioners' sugar and cut into 12 pieces when completely cold and crisp.

COOK'S TIP

The brownie won't be completely firm in the middle when it is removed from the oven, but it will set when it has cooled.

Chocolate Biscotti

Makes 16

INGREDIENTS

1 egg	1 cup all-purpose flour	1³/₄ ounces dark chocolate, roughly chopped
1¹/₃ cup superfine sugar	¹/₂ tsp baking powder	¹/₂ cup toasted slivered almonds
1 tsp vanilla extract	1 tsp ground cinnamon	¹/₂ cup pine nuts

1 Grease a large cookie sheet with butter.

2 Beat the egg, sugar, and vanilla extract in a mixing bowl with an electric mixer until it is thick and pale—ribbons of mixture should trail from the beater as you lift it.

3 Sift the flour, baking powder, and cinnamon into a separate bowl, then sift into the egg mixture and fold in gently. Stir in the chocolate, slivered almonds, and pine nuts.

4 Turn out onto a lightly floured surface and shape into a flat log about 9 inches long and ¾ inch wide. Transfer to the prepared cookie sheet.

5 Bake in a preheated oven at 350°F for 20–25 minutes, or until golden. Remove from the oven and cool for 5 minutes, or until firm.

6 Transfer the log to a cutting board. Using a serrated bread knife, cut the log on the diagonal into

slices about ½ inch thick and arrange them on the cookie sheet. Cook for 10–15 minutes, turning halfway through the cooking time.

7 Cool for about 5 minutes, then transfer to a wire rack to cool completely.

Chocolate Macaroons

Makes 18

INGREDIENTS

2³/4 ounces dark chocolate,
broken into pieces
2 egg whites

pinch of salt
1 cup superfine sugar

1¹/4 cups ground almonds
shredded coconut, for
sprinkling (optional)

1 Grease 2 cookie sheets with a little butter or margarine and line with baking parchment or rice paper.

2 Melt the dark chocolate pieces in a double boiler, then cool slightly.

3 In a mixing bowl, beat the egg whites with the salt until they form soft peaks.

4 Gradually whisk the superfine sugar into the egg whites, then fold in the ground almonds and cooled melted chocolate until all the ingredients are thoroughly incorporated.

5 Place heaping teaspoonfuls of the mixture on the prepared cookie sheets, spacing them well apart, and spread into drops about 2½ inches across. Sprinkle with a little shredded coconut, if desired.

6 Bake in a preheated oven at 300°F for about 25 minutes, or until the macaroons are firm to the touch when pressed with a finger.

7 Cool slightly before carefully lifting the chocolate macaroons from the cookie sheets. Transfer to a wire rack and cool completely before serving.

COOK'S TIP

Store the macaroons in an airtight container and eat within 1 week.

Florentines

Makes 8–10

INGREDIENTS

4 tbsp butter	$1/3$ cup almonds, chopped	2 tbsp candied cherries,
$1/4$ cup superfine sugar	$1/3$ cup chopped candied peel	chopped
$2 1/4$ cup all-purpose flour,	$1/4$ cup raisins, chopped	finely grated rind of $1/2$ lemon
sifted		$4 1/2$ ounces dark chocolate,
		melted

1 Line 2 large cookie sheets with baking parchment.

2 Heat the butter and superfine sugar in a small saucepan until the butter has just melted and the sugar dissolved. Remove the pan from the heat.

3 Stir in the flour and mix until well combined. Stir in the chopped almonds, candied peel, raisins, cherries and lemon rind and mix together well. Place teaspoonfuls of the mixture well apart on the cookie sheets.

4 Bake in a preheated oven at 350°F for 10 minutes, or until lightly golden in color.

5 As soon as the florentines are removed from the oven, press the edges into neat shapes while still on the cookie sheets, using a cookie cutter. Cool on the cookie sheets until firm, then carefully transfer to a wire rack to cool completely.

6 Spread the melted chocolate over the smooth side of each florentine. As the chocolate begins to set, mark wavy lines or the pattern of your choice in it with a fork. Leave the florentines until set, chocolate side up.

Meringues

Makes about 13

INGREDIENTS

4 egg whites
pinch of salt
1/2 cup sugar

1/2 cup superfine sugar
1 1/4 cups heavy cream,
  whipped lightly

1 Line 3 cookie sheets with a few sheets of baking parchment.

2 In a large clean bowl, whisk together the egg whites and salt until they are stiff, using an electric mixer. (You should be able to turn the bowl upside down without any movement from the egg whites.)

3 Carefully beat the sugar into the egg white mixture a little at a time; the meringue should start to look glossy at this stage.

4 Sprinkle in the superfine sugar, a little at a time, and continue beating until all the sugar has been incorporated and the meringue is thick, white, and stands in tall peaks.

5 Transfer the meringue mixture to a pastry bag fitted with a ¾-inch star tip. Pipe about 26 small whirls onto the prepared cookie sheets.

6 Bake in a preheated oven at 250°F for about 1½ hours, or until the meringues are pale golden in color and can be easily lifted off the paper. Let the meringues cool in the turned-off oven overnight.

7 Just before serving, sandwich the meringues together in pairs with the whipped heavy cream and arrange on a serving plate.

VARIATION

For a finer texture, replace the ordinary sugar with superfine sugar.

Index